"Release"

Burt Stuff

RELEASE

RELEASE

Bart Steib

iUniverse, Inc.
New York Lincoln Shanghai

RELEASE

Copyright © 2005 by Bart Steib

iUniverse books may be ordered through booksellers or by contacting:

iUniverse
2021 Pine Lake Road, Suite 100
Lincoln, NE 68512
www.iuniverse.com
1-800-Authors (1-800-288-4677)

ISBN-13: 978-0-595-33853-5 (pbk)
ISBN-13: 978-0-595-78640-4 (ebk)
ISBN-10: 0-595-33853-4 (pbk)
ISBN-10: 0-595-78640-5 (ebk)

Printed in the United States of America

Contents

Acknowledgements

Sister Marie LaReine I.H.M. Thank you for editing this manuscript and as always offering sage advice. Tom Niles, Charles Laniak and Carl Hall offered excellent suggestions and guidance as did Joseph Crivella who designed the cover.

Many thanks to the members of Evergreen Country Club. To Chris and Larry who always supported my efforts. To the WISP group who continue to give back to the sport of golf in their special ways. A special thanks to Dave Kreer and the Edward W.White Council of the Knights of Columbus. Also, to the people at The Williamsburg Deli. Especially, Curtis and Suzy. They were always there to give me support.

I'd also like to thank the faculty of Bishop O'Connell High School and all my students over Thirty-three years who have been a major inspiration for me.

Lastly, I will never forget the teaching encouragement and inspiration of the person about whom I have written this book. Mike Wynn is simply the best teaching Pro I know on the planet. I am deeply grateful for his contributions to this book.

Preface

To a golfer, *release* is the relaxed, fluid movement of the golf club that unleashes the full power and control of the golf swing. When completed properly, the released swing allows the head of the club to reach the ball at the precise moment that the hands, arms, and body of the golfer are perfectly synchronized. Any thought or action of the golfer to attempt to guide, control, or manipulate a golf swing's release usually leads to a missed shot, often explained as too much "hanging on." Thus, only when the golfer has faith enough to unconsciously release his swing can he really understand and sometimes master the elusive, but ecstatic, joy of a solidly struck ball.

Why write a book about release? I have written this book because, in our technological age, the word *release* is a forgotten term, not only in golf but also in life. This book explores the meaning of *release* as it affects the everyday life of one person who has a passion for the game of golf. That passion extends not only to golf, but also to society as well. I am concerned that humanity, like golf, is losing the ability to release. The sense of dance, for instance, seems to be lessened by overreliance on dancing specifics rather than the enjoyment of the freedom of mind and motion within a beautiful musical framework. *Release* is an inner knowing that all pain on a golf course and in life has what I'll call a "glass lightly," shattering the darkness that causes pain. If it doesn't, pain ends up being a "glass darkly." Inner reward isn't the only reason for living. Humanity also needs recognition. The released side of the self appears when the two come together. Above all, release is inner freedom.

Where have the Gene Sarazens, the Jimmy Demarets, the Doug Sanders, or even dancers such as Fred Astaire and Gene Kelly gone? This book is written to challenge those people who believe that *release* is an idea of the past, who believe that golf and life in general are games of power or science. I certainly would agree that technology has made the game more enjoyable for everyone, but can we stop there? Where will the art of the game be in the twenty-first century?

After writing this book, I had an experience, which, at age fifty-eight, brought me again to the meaning of *release* in my life. This experience taught me that in all pain there is a glass lightly; otherwise, pain is a glass darkly. We learn to suffer in God's love on earth. I was playing in the Washington Catholic Athletic Conference Golf Tournament at Breton Bay Golf Club in Leonardtown, Maryland. I was one over par upon reaching the fourth hole, which was designed with a sand trap in the right corner of the dogleg left. Now mind you, I had already finished writing this book, and this is what happened: I teed up, aligning myself with the center of the fairway, thereby blocking out the sand trap on the right. My drive sailed over the sand trap and, to my surprise, went out of bounds. My second tee shot went out of bounds again, as did my third. Finally, I faced my body directly into the woods in desperation, and struck a perfect drive into the center or the fairway. I ended up with an eleven on the hole, putting me out of the tournament, losing by seven shots. Had I disconnected darkness from light, focusing only on the fairway and keeping the sand trap out of my perception? By this I mean, did I make darkness a penance, renouncing myself, and therefore couldn't get my swing out of the penance because I didn't know light was gathering up everything? Truthfully, I wasn't even aware that the light of being in the fairway was bent by the darkness of going into the sand trap. I also might have let my faith in the invisible give power to the darkness in the sand trap. The center of God's will gathers up everything, good and bad. Let good shatter darkness.

A very good friend of mine, Mr. Tom Niles Sr., once told me that when I expressed anxiety over an important putt, I should just putt the ball and believe the power that makes me miss is turned off. He told me that I should believe the putt is already in the hole by trusting that the goodness in making the putt has not yet been bent by the darkness of missing. You might ask yourself, how does that happen? It happens when you understand the meaning of release, and my desire to share that meaning is the reason why I wrote this book.

A few weeks later, I had a dream in which I was playing on a baseball team during my freshman year at the College of William and Mary with a coach named Floyd Tuthill. Coach Tuthill understood the meaning of *release* even when I did not. In the dream, the game was ready to start, but I was somewhere in the stands, talking to friends. When I returned to the dugout, Coach Tuthill told me that he had substituted another player at shortstop for me because I was late. Naturally, I complained, but "Tut" said that I needed to be a team player and to be on time. I accepted his decision, but wondered whom he put in my position, shortstop. The coach had put in Alvin Dark. Alvin Dark? That name stuck in my mind because that was the name of an old Cleveland Indian shortstop. Well, you might ask, what does that have to do with the meaning of *release?* I can only say to you that my dream conceals the answer.

Why should you read this book? Because after you read it, you will be able to figure out the meaning of the dream. And the experience of understanding the symbolism of the dream will release you. The *dream* is an aspect of the glass lightly, swallowing everything in the center of God's will, shattering the darkness. Once released, you will see, as I saw on that day at Breton Bay, that the journey is only beginning.

Such dreams can come from the attention God gives us. God's attention doesn't disturb. Man's attention does. After that day on Breton Bay, I could no longer face my fears. I needed a new understanding. I needed to know that something else was taking me through my panic. I needed to know my journey was into the light, into release. So, read and enjoy my book, and decide for yourself whether you want to live through a journey into the light. Is it possible to keep "release" alive in the twenty-first century? What will be the consequences for our culture if we stop our pursuit and passion for the meaning of release in our lives? This book was written to help you answer these questions. Read, enjoy, and begin to take ownership of your journey into the light.

Beginnings

On July 28, 1999, at 7:35 PM, I was lying on my bed at the Willows Motel in Williamstown, Massachusetts, when I was released! The release came about because I had just shot my best round of golf on a championship course in thirty-five years—a seventy-five!

My friends and I had played at the Taconic Golf Club. The club was owned by Williams College, and it was truly a beautiful course, nestled in the majestic Berkshire Mountains of western Massachusetts. I had been coming to this course for twenty years. On this day, in this round of golf, I experienced release. It was the last day of my two-week vacation to New Hampshire and Massachusetts. For the previous ten days, I had experienced no release.

As I came to learn over the course of that vacation, you can be a hard worker on the same job for thirty years, a married man with a family, a clergyman, or a CEO of a Fortune 500 company, but you may still never experience release.

Golf as Metaphor for Release

For centuries, Western man has said that fulfilling a defined role in a feudal or mercantilist mind-set (i.e., to occupy a traditional role in the day-to-day activities of the world) is the definition of being released. In feudal mind-sets, the attention God gave men disturbed them. Now, however, we know that it's the universe that disturbs us. God released my vision, and my perception of God changed that day on the golf course. I didn't allow God to renounce me, and I didn't see bad shots as penance. Feudal and mercantilist mind-sets don't have the light of faith-based freedom inside them, only a glass darkly. The glass lightly always gives us attention that saves us in a universe that takes focus off ourselves. Golf can be part of that attention God gives us. Why? His attention doesn't disturb us, and can only complement our focus on the game.

The memory of that great round of golf on that wonderful day in July releases me. There was no defined role, no feudal mind-set, no mercantilist ambi-tion—only the freedom of knowing I was dancing with the truth, which kept coming around as long as I didn't give in to the glass darkly inside me. Some-thing about the game of golf has a glass lightly inside it, and I was beginning to feel comfortable with myself as a person who knew there could be a glass lightly as long as I also accepted the glass darkly. It was truly a great feeling, one I wanted to relive again and again because I had discovered something in the game of golf that made me feel different about myself.

Once the people of the twelfth-century understood the proofs for the exist-ence of God as proposed by Thomas Aquinas, they experienced mental release. Did Albert Einstein experience release after he discovered the revolutionary scien-tific principles embodied by the now-famous equation $E = mc^2$? Did these men discover a light that ended all doubt over the existence of light? Is it possible to be connected to that same light on a golf course? I believe that today we are all living in a larger, faster, freer world in which our greatest strength is our greatest weak-ness when we are unaware that we live in a glass darkly and that the universe is an emptying-out experience. The future belongs to those people who have learned to define themselves in a universe that is emptying people out at each moment as a measure of God's will. The universe takes the focus off of the self. It's larger, faster, and freer. We must lose ourselves to find ourselves in the center of God's will, which shatters all darkness. There's nothing we can do that can't be corrected by truth. We don't have to make bad golf shots. God's attention to us shows as good shots. The God of love gives us the inspiration to know that bad shots *might* happen, but they don't have to happen.

Glass Darkly

People who understand the guiding principles in this book will have to be our future leaders. They know there is a truth that is greater than all the resistance inside us—release. We must come to know ourselves as released persons with the potential to accept the glass darkly inside us as part of the water running in our lives, winning our hearts. This is no longer a world in which we can define who we are only by living inside the glass darkly. What is the glass darkly? In golf it is when you let divots, bogeys, sand traps, or water hazards have power over you. We must learn to live with larger hearts because a greater heart without a glass darkly frees us. We must learn to play golf, not with our own heart, but with the heart we anticipate in our dreams, the one we imagine when we envision our perfect game. We play the game not with our hearts, but with the larger heart (God's love), which we believe has golf and everything that already is catching us so we can be released from inside the glass darkly. God's love encompasses all, and to accept this love into our heart opens us, making us receptive to the light that illuminates all that can be. Thus, we live in a world in which we must be open to that which is greater than our own resistance—again, release.

Another thing that golf teaches me is that I need to comprehend that the marathon of life does not have the last word. Sure, we struggle, but there is a larger dream in the struggle that keeps coming alive as we become worthy to receive it. Neither Neil Armstrong, when he walked on the moon; nor Mark McGwire, as he hit his seventieth home run; nor Tiger Woods, upon winning four majors in one year, were plagued by the glass darkly. They didn't listen to the voice that said they couldn't accomplish these feats. They heard the voice trying to be heard without the glass darkly inside it.

On that particular day in Massachusetts, I was released. I was amazed over how golf made me aware of the glass darkly that was already inside me, inhibiting my swing. Nothing I tried to do could control the darkness inside me that was in the glass darkly. I had yet to discover a different zone, one outside the glass darkly, that could recognize the abundance that was already there.

Games

In college, I was not a released person. I played college basketball and baseball, but I was never released. A baseball scout told me that he would have signed me to a contract, if only I had been released. He thought I had the stamina to play only thirty-five or forty games. Of course, I was only nineteen at the time, and I had no idea what he meant by *release.* I didn't have to be released to play forty games, to get a degree from college, to do my job or to be in the Army. But its absence in my life was apparent, even then.

It was then that I began to become aware that some people seemed to live their lives as released human beings. They didn't live for trophies, championships, or promotions, yet they still received these accolades. They seemed to have a work ethic that was a consequence of confidence. The confidence did not come from a fear of failure. And I felt that being near these released people could release me. They had learned to look at things a different way, to find a way to connect the good in themselves with the universe. These people knew the light, which ended all doubt that the light didn't exist.

Stepladder Universe

The truth trying to be heard is the center of God's will, shattering the glass darkly so that your peace on the inside and outside can be released. Upon release, the power of glass darkly is off. Bad shots don't have to happen. In the past, however, bad shots had to happen if you renounced yourself.

Simply put, the stepladder mind-set of the feudal world once blinded people to the truth. When people believed that the planets revolved around the earth, a higher meaning came from believing in a stairway to heaven. When people learned that the planets instead revolve around the sun, a higher meaning was gained by living into the image of the sun king.

It seems to me that it wasn't until Isaac Newton's time that man began to understand that the universe exists outside a larger heart than his own, in a universe in which the heart and mind work cooperatively together. This is the beginning of the acceptance of truth revealed by scientific method. For the first time, the heart of the scientist wasn't his own, but now came out of a larger heart. The scientist could no longer believe just anything he wanted after testing the observations revealed to him by this greater heart. This larger heart, in which humans needed to believe, had eternity and everything man needed to know inside it. When Jesus said we must "lose ourselves to find ourselves," he was speaking of our world today. We can either make the pain of the modern world a glass darkly, or believe that the light in the glass darkly can shatter the pain-causing darkness. It's no longer a world with focus on just one's self. God's attention to you gathers you in the kingdom, a world in which God's attention focuses the self by turning off the power of the glass darkly. God's attention to you holds you in existence. By contrast, any attention man gives causes you to lose focus. God's attention may take an unexpected form. Sometimes, he uses golf to gather you in the kingdom.

Was it the Sacred Heart of Jesus Christ that released me? I think so, but it took golf to introduce to me the idea that a larger heart, made in the image and likeness of God, could transcend the limits of a heart weighted with the worries of a glass darkly. No longer did I perceive a stepladder world into eternity. I now saw an eternity coming out of us in every moment of our lives until we gain the confidence that we are being released. Just as I believe was the case with Isaac Newton, our patient observations can give us confidence that our heaven is continuously coming out of us. It is our covenant with God. Heaven is in the "here" in which everything you were ever going to be is already present in every moment. Imagine learning to swing the golf club from the "here," the present moment with everything you need to know already. The "here" is what makes it all happen in the golf swing, and the "here" is what makes it all happen in life. Without the "here," the modern world is simply too large, too fast, and too free, and it causes too much from the "there" to get into you head when you try to figure it out on your own.

Changing Perspective

This book is about how golf teaches me to break the curse in my heart so that a new heart can release the club. When you finish reading this book, you will likely want more than ever to experience this release. It is better to die than to live without release. What we must learn to do, and what golf is teaching us to do, is to not listen to the voice inside our glass darkly, which says we can't succeed. This will only happen when we realize that a greater heart in God's image and likeness is witnessing to us, which ends all doubt that the good doesn't exist. When that happens, a "you will" attitude replaces an "I can't" attitude, and the fear of saying no to the voice of the glass darkly begins to subside. We begin to trust the light, and in turn the light begins to clarify and illuminate the potential in our game.

The Pro

One person who had this confidence showed me how the game should be played. He showed me that the reason I couldn't play well was because I couldn't release the clubhead. But he didn't start by correcting my grip or stance. He started by demonstrating a ball flight that only a released person could duplicate. Every time this pro hit the ball, it would track to the hole. It just wouldn't lose power. When I hit the same ball from the same spot off the ground, it would lose power. When I asked him how he did it, he only said that you have to release the club if you want the ball to find the hole. When I played basketball and baseball, it only mattered that you made hits or scored points. No one talked about how release affects ball flight.

In golf, you beat yourself up when you aren't released. In baseball, you beat yourself up when you make errors or strike out. It usually occurs when you haven't practiced hard enough. I practiced very hard and didn't often make errors. Remember, however, the scout told me I could play only forty games. In other words, it is possible to practice, score points, hit for a respectable average, and still not be released. The games of life will lie to you when they don't originate in a larger heart inside a universe that empties out. Golf is different because, if you are not released, it will show up in your game, and you will discover how the glass darkly can beat you over and over again. You simply can't control the negative "I can't" voice inside you without the negative continuing to come around. Because the scout said I could only play forty games, I defined myself by the negativity going on inside the glass darkly. When you have this kind of attitude in golf, you always get in your own way. The obvious reason I couldn't play golf as well as I wanted is because I could never get released enough to trust in the good forces that were coming back to me from the other phenomena in the game. Bad shots kept me spiraling downward because the good wouldn't come around. But why?

Coming Alive

I needed to learn to fall upward. By this, I mean that I needed to no longer see golf as just an inner reward with either no self or a self bigger than the game. I now understand it to be a released side of our selves that God uses to gather us into his kingdom. Golf is inside the released side of our selves that receives God's attention. I needed to see everything already present in my swing coming out of my heart in a relationship with the spirit that doesn't annihilate me. But why be annihilated? Golf should release you, and I discovered that the proper attitude of the larger heart in golf is never to annihilate your opponent, but even more important, never to believe that you are being annihilated, because then you are getting in your own way, and that will keep release from happening from inside your larger heart. In other words, to be a released person on the golf course, you have to be guided by a larger heart, not the heart inside yourself with the glass darkly inside it. It means I could never get out of my penance. I could never see the glass lightly in the sand trap or down the fairway. Water and sand were like penances, and pure freedom made me think I was bigger than I was. I didn't know I had a released side of self that used golf to show me God's attention. You must believe in the good will of the greater heart to keep you from believing in the lesser will of the heart with glass darkly inside it. Never give in to the voice that hopes your opponent will miss a big putt. That's what it means to live in the glass darkly. Instead, you must continue to trust in the larger heart, which never reads into your opponent. Empty out that which your larger heart reveals to you, that which you must do on the golf course. You should never run down your opponent, but if you do give in to your negative voice, don't apologize. Just accept that you are emptying out in a larger universe, and let the heart without the glass darkly correct the mistake.

What I've learned in golf is that correcting the mistake without a larger heart keeps you making the same mistakes. It's like you are emptying out to get ahead in the world, not emptying out for the love of the kingdom of God within you. The human heart gets heavier, and the heavier heart is the glass darkly. We must let the heart made in God's image correct our mistakes. That might even mean losing the game until our attitude improves to the point where we let God save us by learning to jump into his arms at every opportunity. To play golf with release, we must allow ourselves to be defined by this larger heart over and over again. For me, faith in God had always meant giving up myself, annihilating myself so that God could use me as his instrument on earth. I couldn't accept the darkness as the mean spirit being emptied out of my heart. Annihilating yourself, however, will never work on the golf course. It keeps you from being a released person and makes you very tense because your faith never tells you that you won't be annihilated if you believe.

My problem was that I always felt that giving myself up meant giving up the world. How could I ever be a released person if I was always stuck in the world because I couldn't give it up without annihilating myself? Well, golf gave me the answer. I began to see that being nothing at my address to the ball didn't mean I was annihilated. It all was present in the "here." I discovered there was no glass darkly. There was no curse. I just had to trust that everything was already in the "here," finishing my swing. "Are we close to understanding release yet?" you may ask. We're getting closer, but we still have more understanding to acquire.

What is the "here" in the golf swing? It is not about everything being already "there," because in that scenario, your swing would be everywhere. And worse yet, you'd start putting the swing in different positions out there to control what's already here. This won't work because that which is here is infinite. It can't be controlled except by believing the swing is already here, finishing. Remember: the "here" is the present moment with everything you need to know already.

My Pro: Mike Wynn

Mike Wynn believed that putting the swing into position keeps you in your own way, causing you to grab the club at impact, thus impeding the finish of the swing. Mike taught me that I needed authority from a larger target to swallow up the glass darkly. The target is larger because Mike says you can never be bigger than the game. The question in release is, how do you give up everything at address and not end up annihilating yourself before you strike the ball? For release to happen, there has to be a belief that when you are nothing at address, you are really something. Golf has taught me that it all originates in the heart, which has its reasons that everyday perception cannot understand. A released heart never gives up, because a larger heart with everything already here inside it won't give up. You have only to accept that when your mistakes are in a glass darkly, you are under a curse.

Believe in a Larger Heart

Keep believing in a larger heart that never annihilates you. If you keep accepting the process of emptying out when you trust, you will begin to see "notes," or signs, projected into your experience that will connect you to the truth. The larger heart saves professional golfers and allows them to "be the ball," as once so aptly, if humorously, described in the classic golf comedy *Caddyshack*. I once met a man from Boyne Mountain Resorts who set up tournaments and exhibitions, and asked him what made the pros so great. He said they all had the fundamentals, but that each pro was a little different, and they knew in their hearts how the larger heart made them different. The fact of the matter is that to live in the "here," you need to be free of the glass darkly. But before you can be so free, you have to live in a larger heart that your faith and trust tells you could never be broken. Golf, in other words, has taught me that there is a "heart" out there that never gives up on our dreams.

Birdies are like dreams on the golf course. Birdies come from the released side of the heart, and the center of God's will uses them to shatter the darkness of bogeys. They are lights waking us up in dreams. The fact of the matter is that our own hearts are in the glass darkly. They are cursed. Our own hearts give up and make mistakes. But we must not reside in our own hearts. Golf teaches us that release is possible when we begin to trust in a greater heart that transcends the heart that can't correct itself.

All my life I have lived in my own heart and have tried to correct all of my mistakes on the golf course. I've rooted against my opponent to win a match. Until I played golf, I never knew there was a heart that was in the "here" and which would correct my mistakes, if I would only believe that the curse was broken. When playing golf through the glass lightly, there is only emptying out and a winning heart. I had never known that golf could come out of a larger heart that I could believe in while I played. For the first time, I began to understand why scouts told me I had no stamina. It was because I had simply never played with faith. I had never played inside a heart that didn't have a glass darkly. Instead, I played with a heart always locked inside a glass darkly, a heart full of fear and doubt, which I was always trying to overcome. I was trying to break the curse by myself without notes.

I began to understand that when you play golf with a new heart, instead of the one with the glass darkly inside it, your game takes on a completely new meaning. You experience something about releasing the club, which gets inside you, and it never lets you give up. You begin to see the "notes from being" connecting you to the truth in the swing. Once you release the club, you never want to give up that feeling. You want to know that release can happen again. It's a feeling akin to a state of grace because you never want to give it up Release is the confidence that keeps you from paranoia. It's knowing you have a released side of self that God uses to gather you for his kingdom. Golf is in the kingdom. The anticipation of release (because the spirit is alive) keeps you from annihilating yourself, and keeps you striving even while you are giving up in your own heart, giving up in such a way that you gain a new heart that won't give up on you.

I believe that golf is a work from the Father that has faith inside it. In other words, to fully realize the potential in your golf game, you need a relationship with Jesus Christ, who reveals the heart of the Father on the golf course. It is not possible to have a relationship to the Lord that annihilates golf. That would put a style of golf in your own heart in which annihilating your opponent is the key to success. A faith of annihilation never makes the jump into the new heart. A relationship with the Lord can help you to resist these tendencies and can produce a wonderful experience on the golf course that can release you.

The right "here," then, is the key ingredient if you are ever going to reach a point at which you can believe in a state of grace and repeated release, where the glass darkly will still be there but only in your old heart with the dark voice that won't accept emptying out due to insecurity. There won't be a new heart when all things are possible. The water, sand traps, and rough can be experienced as emptying out your old heart. No longer will you have to read sand traps and hazards into your next shot, because you will begin to sense being released by your new heart in the emptying out of your old heart in the notes.

As I opened my heart, I began to witness myself and the phenomena of a new heart; my good swings could connect to the authentic swings that were already present in my being. Golf saved me because it doesn't lie or deceive. For a time, I almost quit because I couldn't stop the negative from coming around inside my old heart, which was full of darkness. When playing golf feels like you're doing time in a prison, you don't even want to play. Release shatters that glass darkly.

Golf became a way out for me because, not only did it not lie to me, but it showed me a way to know whether I was released, and it showed me when I was released. It even began to show me heaven in my soul. I was no longer headed into eternity on a stepladder. On the golf course, heaven could come out of me if I trusted in the "here."

Recognizing the Voice

In the modern world, where the focus is taken off the self, we must see faith-based freedom shattering the darkness so our game will speak up as if it's a voice. The voice is what moves us.

At this point in my journey, I asked myself whether it was golf that released me, or whether it was existence as a released person who played golf that allowed me to find the right path. Maybe golf was something a higher power used to make me aware of my weakness. If I made golf part of my phenomena, so that the good in the game could come around, I would begin to see the heart in golf that doesn't have a glass darkly, the heart that isn't cursed. The voice that says traps are in the way no longer has a hold over me, because I know the fairways and the greens exist in a larger heart than my own. I just had to learn to accept the inevitable emptying out that has to occur if the game is larger than we are.

For the first time, I didn't have to define myself by the voice inside my glass darkly when I played golf. I began to realize that golf could be a part of the phenomena that is greater than my resistance. There would still be a glass darkly, but it would no longer be controlled by the limits of the stepladder mentality. Limits could now be a product of a glass darkly, and they failed to change my heart. I had to get the abuse out of my heart and begin to see a new heart through a glass lightly in my swing. I began to see that you can't play golf with the stepladder in your mind-set, because a feudal mind-set gets its strength from an old "heart," and it fails to understand the game in a manner coming from a new heart without a glass darkly—a heart that doesn't have a curse. In a larger, faster, freer world, you simply can't control the power in your old heart without your limits becoming hot spots in your game. *Hot spots* are the situations in a round of golf when you go blind under pressure and miss shots. They occur when you don't trust the released side of your self.

So, to be *released* means to find that strength that keeps the power from becoming a hot spot. It means to find that you play the game with a larger heart, called "release." It's to begin to discover how you can get out of your own way.

Mike Wynn: Teaching Me Release

One person who never gets in his own way on the golf course is the pro who taught me about ball flight, Mike Wynn. He teaches and plays golf at Fauquier Springs Golf Club in Warrenton, Virginia. He is the only pro who emphasized that release is the starting point of the golf swing. Mike taught me that golf can teach us that release is possible, not only on the course, but also in life. "Golf," Mike says, "is not a game which you can play with a lot of thinking going on inside your head." Golf, for Mike, is all about learning to trust your instincts. The "sacred" knows who you are. The sacred knows you can swing, so trust that the good in the phenomena can connect to your inner rhythm and that your swing can become more authentic. Mike taught me that golf is in the heart without the glass darkly, the heart in which you can dream your shots while you are making them. Golf, Mike says, is best played where there are no hands on the club at impact. Most people hang on with at least six figurative hands. Fear and tension cause you to grip the club with six hands. Golf, however, is meant to be a game played with no hands. No one before Mike had ever told me that a reality can already be present in the world that does not have a glass darkly inside it. Golf is that kind of reality. My world, up until the time I met Mike Wynn, was always defined by the glass darkly inside me, a negative voice that said my dreams could never be on earth—a kind of cursed worldview. As a result, I couldn't get released, not even by correcting my mistakes in the glass darkly. The curse would always get in the way. I couldn't accept the emptying out and the notes that were needed to break the curse.

But suppose there are no mistakes, suppose there are only dreams to be fulfilled. Golf teaches you that dreams can be fulfilled, that release can mean that all the things he created are shining. John 14:10 speaks of the works of the Father, and how the works of the Father are within us: "Believest thou not that I am in the Father, and the Father in me? The words that I speak unto you I speak not of myself: but the Father that dwelleth in me, he doeth the works."

For a long time, I thought the works of the Father were in creation. Well, suppose you and I are also part of those works. That means that what God meant to do with us is being revealed to us freely, like the finish of the swing formed in the image and likeness of God. Here, when you release your swing, you begin to experience resting in God because God rested on the seventh day after he gave us the game of golf from his heart. Experiencing release enables eternity to come out of us right at the proper moment. From golf, we learn that everything we want to comprehend about ourselves is an awakening dream that teaches us that our eyes are always open.

Learning to Jump

This new attitude tells me that everyone is called to be released. To be released means that the works of the Father, which include golf, have already been completed. We can choose. They have been completed, but they are intertwined between a glass lightly and a glass darkly. We can choose to stay in a glass darkly until pain destroys us, or we can choose to be released in a glass lightly. Release is knowing that a released side of ourselves exists. We just have to jump into the heart where these works have been completed, and begin to observe our dreams unfolding from this new heart.

The problem, of course, is that there are sand traps and hazards which tell you there are no dreams, there is no larger heart catching you. You have to accomplish these works with your own heart. There is no larger heart correcting your mistakes, because what needs to be done was already completed by the seventh day. So, on the golf course every shot you make is an example of how the works of the Father have already been completed in your game. With each step on the course, you begin to experience being caught. The game, with all its ecstasy, has the feeling of a glass lightly shattering the doubts and fears that make bad shots so you know that the momentum could always be there. It might not be there, but release means you believe it is there. The game kidnaps you (in a good way), so that you want to believe in your heart that your next shot is a work from the Father. You begin to play in a new heart, where your mistakes have already been corrected. You stop playing in your heart of darkness in a larger, faster, freer world.

Hence, until I met Mike Wynn, I never knew it was possible to play sports without a glass darkly inside, without a curse. There could always be a light at the end of the tunnel that was not part of our greatest resistance. The trick in golf is to try to learn how to transcend those places that hold you back. Actually, the game itself will do that for you when you see the fairways and greens as releasing you, inside the emptying out of the bunkers and hazards trying to stop your dreams.

The trick to understanding release in golf is knowing, like Mike Wynn, that there are no bad swings. Something from the works of the Father restored by

Christ already corrects your swing, even when you think you have made a mistake. That's the jump you have to make, to believe that the Father doesn't make junk if you persevere in jumping. Jumping is simply believing that what is already finished by the works of the Father will catch you in a swing that can't make mistakes. Learn to trust your released side of self.

A Distant Light

The knowledge of myself that knows I am inside the center of God's will—which gives me authority to keep going because the light at the end of the tunnel erases all mistakes—is the ecstasy-released side of oneself.

I've learned that our own hearts can make mistakes, but that, if we believe in a greater heart correcting them, as we make them, we will be released by the light at the end of the tunnel. Golf has taught me that I no longer have to fear being broken down on the course. I merely have to play my game in a larger heart trusting with each shot that there is a light at the end of the tunnel, until there is no tunnel. I will still make mistakes, but I will stop worrying about correcting them. They have already been corrected by the works of the Father and restored to us by our Lord's death on the cross. And these works, like our shots, are our dreams; with these great works of the Father restored in Christ, we can finally say no to the glass darkly inside us, and be corrected by a greater heart as we learn to trust him in all his ways of emptying us out. It doesn't mean we don't make mistakes; it just means that there is a greater heart always there, even when mistakes are made. This greater heart is the light at the end of a tunnel, which will erase everything.

The key to playing golf is to play the course while staying out of the hot spot, that place in the glass darkly that pushes the button that erodes confidence. It is to learn to recognize a reality of the sacred that might keep our lives from becoming a hot spot. Is that reality of the sacred in the golf swing? Is that the key to being released?

The Swing

Mike Wynn says the swing is a motion we can't feel, but which we always try to perfect. Why can't we feel the motion? Mike says that the moment we try to feel the motion, the body becomes a part, and instead of swinging the clubhead, the body ends up controlling the swing. This causes a great reduction in clubhead speed. When that happens, all the parts of the swing aren't moving together to a more perfect union in the clubhead. "Remember," Mike said, "the swing is a motion we can't feel because everything—all parts—are working together." What Mike was saying was that *release is all the parts working together in a more perfect union that you can't feel, because then all the parts wouldn't be together.* It's almost like the swing is an orchestra that you conduct. When the parts are working independently, you begin to sense the music of the swing—the light at end of tunnel that erases all mistakes. When that happens, you release your dark side when it comes out because you know it's already released inside the released side of self.

When any part of the body—shoulders, hands, or hips—starts the swing, you are immediately lost because the body becomes a part, and with the body controlling the swing, the clubhead doesn't. When the body controls the swing, the clubhead can't release, because the more perfect union with the clubhead, which is always present, is now fragmented by feeling rather than knowing. For Mike, that authentic swing is always present to the golfer, if the golfer believes in a sacred reality, which is the "here." What Wynn believes is that, for a more perfect union to happen, you have to trust the motion of the swing you are always trying to perfect. You can trust the motion of the swing because it's already here even before you start swinging. That is why you can't feel the motion of the swing. You wouldn't be trusting what is already here if you had to feel it. Essentially, it's a leap of faith to believe it's already here when you accept that you are nothing at address. Nothing, not because the works of the Father haven't created you, but nothing because everything you are ever going to do in the swing is already here finishing God's work from the beginning of creation. You really have to reach a point where it's in this region of the heart. It's in this region where the arms, legs, and body swing.

What I have learned from golf is that, with the proper attitude, my mistakes are already erased. Even if I make bad swings, they have already been corrected by the works of the Father, and by the restoration of those works in Jesus Christ.

For six years, Mike Wynn, who is five feet, five inches tall, played on the pro tour. Why didn't his career go longer? For Mike, it became difficult to combine the demands of golf with the responsibility of raising a family. Remember, you have to trust your swing before the clubhead can release itself. Mike saw the works of the Father catching him in a free college education, a family, and a career. Is it possible to be released in all three areas by believing faith is catching you? Again, the light at end of tunnel has released everything negative, so Mike "plays" his way through life with a released attitude. Negative things happen, but the glass lightly target always releases you. You have to let it be, or your pain will be a glass darkly. Does faith catch you in your total life the way your swing catches you? For golfers like Mike, all the parts will release themselves into a more perfect union only when you learn to jump and trust that you are being caught by everything already there, finishing the work the Father had started.

This is why golf is such a great game for the twenty-first century. It points all of us to the need all humans have to be unbound, to have our lives overhauled, and to have our hearts changed, transformed.

Ending the Glass Darkly

Anyone who plays golf can feel his own slavery to the glass darkly inside the human condition. The trick is not to let the glass darkly become a hot spot on the golf course. Golf can teach us that there is an authenticity to the swing which is without limits, because when you swing with the union of the phenomena inside you, it unleashes a power that you feel is not your own, but at the same time is your authentic swing. You must learn to trust release even when it is not there because that means you are trusting inside the emptying out of the universe, which is bigger than you are. You have to be patient with yourself, knowing you won't be annihilated by the unknown, which is already here on the inside of your heart. Is the unknown with everything already present in a relationship to golf, or in a relationship to golf in eternity? This is a key question, because how you answer it will determine whether you play the game in your heart or in the larger heart where everything is already present in what you observe. It is not just a visual observation you are making each time you learn something new in the golf swing.

Release is when you experience the parts of the swing in you that have been there from the beginning in the works of the Father at the beginning of creation. But to be released, you have to get into the swing. Mike says you have to admit that you are fighting something, and admit that there is a glass darkly inside you that needs to be restored by the works of the Father in Jesus Christ. How can you do that, you might ask, when your mistakes have already been corrected, already been forgiven?

Admitting Denial

If golf has taught me that self matters, then what has always been here will be made known to me if I allow myself to receive it. So what keeps us from receiving what is already here? Mike says we don't trust in release because we are in denial. Hence, we must admit denial and allow the unknown from inside us to release what is already here. And what's already here is golf being a work of the Father releasing me. This idea applies to all aspects of life. We must trust a higher power to release us. If release isn't here, or the desire to be released, the self that matters will stay in the glass darkly, in the curse that can't be broken without notes from being.

Breaking the Curse

Never releasing your released side of self is a glass darkly: never getting out of glass darkly, doing time, not being able to turn it around—no inspiration moving you. We must learn to allow release from the world of the Father to break the curse. We break it by accepting emptying out, not denying it, and then letting truth guide us. The question is, how do we know the works of the Father that correct our mistakes are not just observations that keep us at a fork in the road? You must learn to accept emptying out at your fork in the road and learn to trust the notes that being is revealing to you. What are these "notes"? The center of God's will inside you, which gives you authority, has notes that are personal if you let the authority of God gather you in.

Mike might say that people who play in a certain way could be better if they acknowledged they were fighting something. But what Mike also says is that fighting something means a game bigger than you are is correcting your swing. Acknowledging that you are fighting something is accepting emptying out. You want to accept the Lord's love, ending the agitation of the hour of death.

For example, at times in golf, you hit forks in the road—which club to choose, which shot to take. Can you jump, keep believing you never make a mistake, and wait for the flow to correct your shots? Well, you might wait for the flow, but if you don't acknowledge that the flow corrects your mistakes, what you think is the flow or release might be empowering a glass darkly inside you. You still think you have a debt to pay. You don't trust the "rising"—seeing the notes rise out of the darkness until all the darkness is erased.

How do you know that the observations that release you are works of the Father? They might deceive you if your flow doesn't come from the soul that is always there when you trust in your heart that what you are fighting is the flow correcting your swing. Well, you aren't deceived if you accept that you are flowing in the truth of your notes. The notes are personal from the Father.

A Self That Matters

The mystery of the game of golf is that, unless you are aware you are emptying out and that emptying out is not a curse, the hour of death will rule you. Again, when life is penance you can't get out—you have no authority from God inside and out. You have to decide whether you want to keep doing time.

Golf has taught me that I fight the love of God inside me and around me, and that I need to be released. Golf has taught me that it's possible to be released, that it's possible to have a self that matters, that I don't have to live in an hour of death all of my life, and that it's possible to face my fears. Golf has also taught me that release is possible for only those people who admit they have fears, or at least admit they are not all they can be, but also realize that what they are fighting is the good will of the Father in Jesus bringing them home inside the emptying out of his cross. The glass lightly says you are not in an hour of death. When people don't admit they are fighting the glass lightly with their hour of death inside them, release isn't possible because they are in the hour of death and don't know it. The big picture can't release them! It becomes almost like a mindless existence. The idea is to accept the emptying out so the glass darkly won't become a curse.

Some people think they are bigger than God. That is why—to attain release at higher levels—there must always be an admission that emptying out is necessary before you can swing the club properly. Release can happen only when we open our hearts to a higher power that releases us by giving us the sense that we don't need to agitate ourselves to make the complete swing. We only have to accept emptying out when we notice we are agitated. The swing without agitation is inside the works of the Father. How do we know? Because release teaches us that what we are fighting is really the lack of trust that the works of the Father are already present in the swing. When we have ambition coming from a greater heart, we have a chance of being released.

If we don't acknowledge the original sin, the glass darkly, or the negative voice inside us, we might stay in the flow, but our swings, and our lives, will always burden us with selfishness. To be complete, we'll never live the impossible dream, because we will live in denial that the works of the Father are releasing us. Emptying out will be lacking in our swings. Why? Because we wouldn't need wholeness or being to give us the notes we need inside our emptying out. People who play golf without an inner knowing (which releases them) never experience the heart of the game, which is always present when you admit that you needed to empty out for the love of God to learn your swing.

A Larger Power

You have to acknowledge something larger than you. Your wholeness is always rising from within your complete being. Do you have to fall first before you admit that you are nothing? I think that's the glass darkly, the original sin, which is telling us we have to fall. Release is what keeps the fall from having any power over us when we accept emptying out whatever is befalling us. What golf has taught me is that we don't have to listen to that glass darkly, which says we have to fall. We just have to accept that emptying out the glass darkly makes us complete.

Original sin is Adam's putting the fall of man inside everyone, making us think that we have to fight God to grow. On the golf course, we will see that we can't dwell on the fall if we want to play good golf, but we have to admit that getting power from always falling is what we are fighting. Thus, accepting our fighting means we are accepting emptying out. It means we are emptying out so we can see that the light of the works of the Father at the beginning of creation is what makes us whole. I've learned this from the game of golf. We can be released before we die, by a light that keeps pain from robbing us of our destiny. A heart that has daylight—and not death—inside it has no angst. How? When we realize that fighting occurs because we think it is necessary for our true hearts to come out of our selves, that's when we make mistakes. Golf teaches us that a stream that has paid all our debts runs inside our being when we learn to accept emptying out and trust the notes that being gives us to discover the truth about ourselves.

Trust

At this point, I must discuss the meaning of trust in the golf swing. Chandler Harper, a renowned pro golfer, told Mike Wynn that you have to trust your swing. You have to trust that your authentic swing is already here and is always releasing you when you accept that emptying out is necessary to complete your swing. Ideally, we play golf as if through a glass lightly. We must learn to release the curse of our heart's original sin. Release doesn't search out your heart; the spirit asks you how long you want to live in the hour of death. To paraphrase St. Paul, we have to learn to play knowing the abundance is already here, even if we don't see it right now. We have to learn to be invisible, waiting on release to heal us while daylight searches out our hearts. What we are fighting goes all the way back to the Garden of Eden. What we are fighting is disbelief in the works of the Father, shattering our negative opinion of ourselves. We just have to get the fall out of our minds and let fighting our dreams be replaced by a trust that Jesus has already shattered the darkness when we accept emptying out.

Mike says that playing golf should be effortless, a totally released exercise, because we know our mistakes have been corrected. Our dream is still alive, just as before, if we totally allow ourselves to be released by learning to be invisible, with no hands on the club at impact. That's why I play golf. That's why it is such an attraction. To play well is to be released. The freedom in golf, I believe, is what draws all people to the game.

Release is inner freedom. When I talk about trust in golf, what I am really doing is talking about learning to trust freedom. I am learning to run to daylight until I realize daylight has been there all along. The golf swing frees me. When pros talk about the swing, what they do is get out of their own way. Golf teaches them that you can't exert control over the game because the game will always be bigger than we are, inside a sacred universe. If we could control the game, we would be risking having our greatest strengths becoming our greatest weaknesses. Golf teaches that the abundance of good swings is already present when we stop fighting, and begin to practice knowing that the works of the Father have already been completed, even when we are finishing the works. Release, then, is knowing that the truth is always making itself known, even when we miss shots. We just have to trust our notes when we make the next shot. Golf teaches us a passion for life, which becomes the bottom line with the Lord's word inside your passion. For me, golf is part of a letter that the Lord has been writing to me from the beginning of creation. My passion is anticipating that which comes next in the letter. I ask myself, what note is being sending to me that will reveal the truth about myself?

Hence, before you can succeed in golf, you have to trust that the abundance is already present. When you miss a shot, the abundance is still there, but it is a cloudy abundance, clouded by the glass darkly keeping you from your abundance, clouded by the sense that there is not knowing in your shot. Without a knowing, you will either make the shot or you will miss. How do you know the knowing is in the shot? Release. Simply, you have absolute trust that what is already "here" is finishing. The "here" swings everything out there. But there is a vital mystery here. Because Adam and Eve fell, we are fighting something. The good news is that the fighting is not caused by daylight breaking into our darkness. The fighting is the curse that needs to be broken in every person. What is meant by God and the game being bigger than we are is that God creates golf to share his freedom with us.

In the larger, faster, freer universe of Einstein, Freud, and Gates, we can no longer make religion an enemy of the world. We just have to admit that God and his universe are bigger than we are if we want to be free and we have to accept emptying out so the truth in the notes will set us free. There is no way of having a low handicap or of traveling the high road without acknowledging that the glass darkly is robbing you of your peace, unless you see the abundance as God sharing his freedom with us. We will not see how the abundance can take the cloudiness out of us and leave us with the light that has always been there. You see, the game of golf in the sacred universe is supposed to end all doubt that the abundance is there. It truly is there. I've learned that the task is to believe in every shot. In every moment there is nothing to correct; only everything already being released can correct your misses, and only by jumping and trusting can you be released.

Wholeness as Discipline

Tiger Woods hit a poor shot at the first hole of Arnold Palmer's tournament in Bay Hill, Florida. But when Tiger got his ball, he didn't allow his poor shot to be a glass darkly or a thorn in his flesh. Tiger understood that his wholeness from the works of the Father inside him was what completes the shot. He only needed to believe. His next shot will always be his best shot because he knows that even if the abundance is cloudy, when you believe the power is off, the light that is always on will help you understand that, when you jump, all will be light. This is a light in the darkness, because you know that what you are fighting does not mean you are fallen, it means you have to let go and let the works of the Father release you from your personal war. In a sense, golf has taught me that it's possible to be a beautiful "hurricane" if you accept what you are fighting and believe the fighting is the light waking up your heart to believe. The hour of death is not inside you when you trust God loves you with passion, and passion for God's love is what the intellect follows.

You see, Tiger Woods has holes in his being, just like the rest of us, but he doesn't allow the hour of death to be a reason why he makes good shots. He doesn't make his mistakes a curse for his next shot. When you do that, you have holes in your being, and golf ends up being a game played in a bucket of water that leaks. When the glass darkly is the focus of your game, you will be undermined by a thorn in the flesh. Tiger has bad shots, but his bad shots just happen. I believe that reality for Tiger is always about his good shots. Reality for Tiger has no limits, no thorns in the flesh, no glasses darkly because he believes the light releasing him is ending the abuse he feels when he keeps opening his heart to the works of the Father.

Golf Discipline

For Tiger Woods, golf discipline means learning to accept bad shots until good shots replace them. It means never giving up on the possibilities for glory, which are always there, when we allow release to correct our mistakes.

The ability to discern what is in a room of light from what is in a world of darkness makes it possible to be on our way to being released. We are open to what it meant to trust. For Mike Wynn, trust is the cornerstone of the golf swing. I know I've said this before, but sometimes in my book, and in life, you have to watch the movie more than once to get the most out of it. We must trust that when we play the course, the power of the glass darkly is already off. In Mike's definition, the swing is a motion you can't feel, yet you are always trying to perfect. But golf has taught me that the heart you are trying to perfect is the one that believes that everything is already here, finishing your swing for you. It's the heart that never gives up on the swing being able to finish when you believe in your heart that there are no mistakes in your swing to correct. When you finally begin to accept that release and emptying out is what is correcting your mistakes, you will begin to experience a motion that is like the wind. Hence, it's release that is like the wind that I want to move toward as I listen to the thoughts of Mike Wynn.

Motion in the Swing

Remember, Mike says the swing is a motion you can't feel, yet you are always trying to perfect it. You can't feel it because it's a matter of knowing where your hands are on the club. Not feeling, because being attached to the club enslaves you and causes you to grab the handle at impact. There is no freedom swinging the club if it isn't based on knowing. For centuries, human beings attached their heads and the world to themselves. Man was the measure of all things, Protagoras of Abdera said, so all things were attached to man so reality could in effect be controlled by man, logic, and systematic thought. But notice that in logic and systematic thought, there is no heart with everything already here finishing the works of the Father. On the golf course I am learning that the abundance of good shots is all part of a language I speak with God, so that I know I am not alone. The trick to being released is to play the course and not attach any meaning to your bad or good shots. Just trust that continual communication with your spirituality will keep your self from being alone.

This is the critical issue of modern times. We have no control over reality. Any attachments of any kind could turn on us, could leave us empty. We must, in our world today, learn to communicate so we are not left alone in the box of what we are attaching to ourselves. In fact, the fourteenth century mind-set, with its spirituality somewhere else, could be alone in today's world. Unless you are out of the box today, unless you let God add substance to your freedom in an unintended way, you will never be free. You will always be attached and will always be attaching. You will be ego driven, and that's death on the golf course, because the works of the Father have no heart inside them. Works without faith are dead. Your golf game will be dead, with no life.

In this world today, we must have faith in the works of the Father on the golf course so we will not be alone, but rather will have that communication that says we are not alone. Knowing is freedom. The modern world demands that we know not in our hearts but in our heart of hearts. All the works are already finishing in your heart when you swing the club. You must understand how everything is already here swinging your arms. You don't have to feel where your hands and arms are in the swing. You already know that your hands and arms are in your heart when you finish the swing in your heart. There is a kind of knowing that your hands and arms are where they are supposed to be, because you know even when you can't see them that they are in your heart. They are the works of the Father you must learn to trust by faith.

The Swing

So even though you can't feel the motion of the swing, you can know you're swinging. You don't have to attach your swing to your body; you must attach your body and swing to faith. You just know where all the positions are in your swing. How do you know? What you know is that you get out of the glass darkly by learning to accept emptying out as the pathway to the light at the end of the tunnel, shattering your illusions. The light flows through the swing, but again, the swing isn't the light.

What is the light which flows through the swing that you can't feel? The motion that Mike says flows through the swing, which you can't feel, is *release.* Release, because at the moment of impact the power is off. The light completes the swing. When Mike says you are fighting something, he wants you to know that what you are fighting is the glass darkly, which doesn't want to empty out so light can show up in your swing.

When receiving a golf lesson from Mike, he'll talk about mechanics like other pros. But mechanics for Mike won't be release. At the same time, release is not without mechanics. For Mike, the mechanics that produce release come with the motion. The focus, for Mike, is the motion, not the ball. For Mike, the motion is not about mechanics, it's about discipline. However, discipline is not about what we traditionally call control. Discipline, for Mike, is focused attention. Focused attention means developing a swing that is consistent and won't break down under pressure, and maintaining trust that good shots will replace the bad shots.

We are all familiar with the difficulty John Daly has had in getting control of his swing on the golf course. He has a difficult time controlling the high octane that is part of his disposition. Control is a bad word for Mike when speaking about discipline in the swing. Mike says control can be the thorn in the flesh that inhibits your swing. What are you controlling? Are you attaching yourself to discipline because you have yet to figure out that you live in a larger, faster, freer world? Are you afraid to be alone? For Mike, in the modern world, being alone means learning to fall upward so you can know the "here" that is already present and already finished. You must experience the communication with the works of the Father through Mike, who God uses to make his relationship to you personal.

When you receive a lesson from Mike, it's all about communication. What you experience during the lesson is how communication with Mike about the swing is about not being alone in the universe. Mike never attaches himself to you during the lesson. It's his ability to communicate release with no hands on the club, his ability to give you a sense of knowing and a sense of freedom, a sense that in your emptying out, being is revealing to you the trust about yourself and your swing. The heart in the knowing is the release, and the release is the sense that you are not alone in the communication. It is as if, when the student is ready, the teacher appears. Mike is that type of teacher who has the answer that always gets your hands off the club so you know you are not alone. The light says you are not alone. Hence, Mike believes you should let go because you are not alone. Release will catch you. Keep emptying out when you reach a fork in the road and the light will catch you. Mike would want John Daly to let his octane out more so release could catch him. God is good. Trust the spirituality given you to catch you when you empty out.

Fall Upward

You have to see life as having glass lightly moments. Take voting rights, for example, or anything that says to us, "It doesn't have to be this way." Just living with things as they are, instead of as they could be, is not falling upward. Falling upward is knowing you don't have to go downward. It's a choice you make. You can believe in the future or stay in the glass darkly. Given the choice, you should believe you have a released side of self.

Mike would not want John Daly to see his problems as obstacles he has to jump over to get to the light, or to jump over by controlling his dark side. No, Mike wants his students to believe release is shattering our obstacles. What we need to do in our hearts is get out of our own way by emptying out so the glass lightly can penetrate our glass darkly. As you experience the glass lightly, you get a sense that you want the spirit to keep talking to you. There is never a lesson from Mike where I don't want him to keep talking to me. It's this sense that someone there is talking to us that releases us and says we are not alone. So Mike would tell us to fall upward in our swings. Experience the power of release catching you, and believe that your spirituality is release, rather than control. Heaven is over you now, breaking into your dark side.

Many students come to Mike in denial, because they still have the mind-set that attaches the world to the self and separates the spirituality of release from the self. They still base not being alone on attaching their minds, hearts, and souls to themselves, and this prevents release from catching them. How can release catch you when you already have the answer and don't experience the grace shattering the darkness? Hence, when Mike instructs his students, he first makes the assumption that they are fighting something, and that's why they are getting the lesson. They are in a glass darkly and don't know it. What are they fighting? Pressure. People can't live without pressure because they can't accept the truth of their condition. It means we all have a glass darkly inside us, but it can have light of God inside it. And what is the truth? St. Paul said, "No one is righteous, no, not one." The truth is, we all have a thorn in the flesh, and that means accepting emptying out as part of the human condition. Golf teaches us that emptying out can be the path for the light to show up in our game.

There is a released side of self that God is using to gather us in and shatter our glass darkly side. Vijay Singh said, after he lost to Tiger Woods in THE PLAYERS Championship (2001), that on the fourteenth hole a bad swing happened. He doesn't look at good things just happening. Good things for Vijay are what really happen. It's a bad shot that just happens. When you aren't released, it's impossible to see good things happening. We don't have to go through a glass darkly to get to the birdie. The glass darkly is there but the light, the fairways, and the greens are always here, so we can learn to believe that it's possible to swing a glass lightly.

We don't need bunkers to know we are fighting something. Original sin tells us there are bunkers. We just have to learn to see the bunkers as emptying us out so the glass lightly can show up from inside our hearts. And what is inside us will become the notes from being inside our hearts that shatter the darkness. When we learn to believe in that communication, our faith will end all doubt that the glass lightly hasn't always been with us. The interior communication, with our trust in the works of the Father, will be what keeps us from feeling alone on the golf course. We will no longer be disappointed by our bad shots because, like Vijay Singh, we will know that bad shots only happen. Reality is the glass lightly over us all around the course. For years I have fought the battle with the glass darkly, not knowing that it is the light trying to break through, correcting all of my mistakes when I accept emptying out my bad shots as not real. It has always been in the way when I pursue my dreams, but the good news is that it isn't real.

Even in my faith it has tried to make the Mass unreal. Yes, I understand from golf that I no longer have to do penance, and that "doing time" is part of going to Mass. It keeps Mass in the glass darkly and doesn't shatter the darkness that causes the glass darkly. Mass begins to lose its meaning in a glass darkly, when I know that Mass should have an authority inside me and around me as a celebration with God. Now, I know the Mass is the glass lightly filling up my heart when I accept emptying out as a pathway to truth, not a curse. Just as the good shots on the golf course keep the glass lightly over me, I know that the Mass and the golf course and all of creation are over me and coming out of me because my faith in the word of God is all about the works of the Father being inside me and outside me.

Golf Is Teaching

Golf teaches that you can never control the glass darkly in yourself on the golf course. We must learn to accept it as the light breaking through to us so we will empty out our hearts and let the light end the power abuse has over you. Controlling the thorn in your flesh only puts holes in your good swings, so that you never play the game in the light. What happens is that your negative mind-set always ends up getting you in your own way on the course because you never anticipate anything good ever happening. The good news, however, is that golf can teach you that there truly is a reality where greens and fairways come out of you and you come out of greens and fairways. The question is, where do you get the trust in your heart?

That is what faith in Jesus Christ teaches you on the course. By his death and resurrection, we have been set free. He is the savior of the world. On the golf course, when you see hazards, bunkers, and rough, you are not seeing with the heart of Jesus. You are not seeing with heaven over you. I have learned that whenever I put myself down or am reminded of my weaknesses, I am lacking in faith that Jesus has overcome the world. I don't have to remind myself that I miss shots to know that I am fighting something. But I do have to accept that fighting something is emptying out, not a curse. What I need to do is know that the works of the Father are correcting me. The glass lightly is inside me shattering darkness because release was not inside me and I could only know that bad shots happen. As long as I keep being reminded of the glass darkly not being in the glass lightly, it's impossible to stop fighting myself on the course.

We must keep opening our hearts and trusting. The power of darkness is broken when we are convinced light is shattering darkness. Then and only then can our emptying out be over. The darkness will still be there in the kingdom, but we know we can beat the odds. Golf is teaching me that there is a reality coming from inside me and connecting to the works of the Father around me, which says that accepting that I am emptying out is part of getting into the light. We need to know God puts shots in our path for us to play. A glass lightly, which you learn to see with your heart, ends all fighting.

Learning the Heart

Golf can teach you that all creation is waking up in your heart. The waking up in your heart is an authority you get in your game that has freedom inside it. You own your game. Ben Hogan owned his game. You know the released side of your self owns your game. In fact, what I would like you to see is how everything waking up is already inside, so that when we learn from Mike Wynn how everything is already inside, we can trust that all parts of the swing are waking up.

Do you remember John 14:10, which I quoted earlier? Golf can teach you that the works of the Father in the golf swing can give the golfer a heart that wakes up creation inside him, so that like Jesus, the golfer can be inside the Father, and the Father can be inside the golfer. When that happens, is it possible we can believe that it's possible that a glass lightly is ending forever the fighting inside all creation? What release points all of us toward is the meaning that is inside the heart of Christ when we see how the swing is inside us and we are inside our swings. This communication, I believe, is the deeper awareness we need to have if our lives are ever going to be released.

But before you can know this deeper communication in the golf swing, Mike says, you first must admit in your heart that you are fighting something. Maybe it's a pull hook, a slice, or a shank. However, you can only own your game if it comes from attention God gives you. Remember, admitting you are fighting something starts to cure the hook, the slice, and the shank if you learn to listen to the swing in your heart which is emptying out the pull, the slice, and the shank. The light we must learn to trust is always shattering the darkness on the course. We must learn to believe the water is always running so the emptying out won't be a problem.

Balance

Sometimes, as I did, you need a pro like Mike Wynn to show you your swing without a glass darkly inside it. How could Mike help you? He couldn't if you didn't trust his knowledge of the game. He is not saying you can't learn from other pros, but if he is the pro who can see your swing without a thorn in the flesh, then you better trust him to get the glass darkly out of your swing. When you can't trust, you are unable to release. What is it you need to trust in the golf swing without a glass darkly? For Mike, you need to trust balance. For Mike, however, balance doesn't mean not falling off your feet. As Mike sees it, you might not fall off your feet, but that doesn't mean you are balanced. For Mike, balance means being able to maintain your height from the start to the finish of the swing. It means never diving into the ball with your body so your arms aren't away from you to the finish of your swing. When that happens, the body doesn't maintain height, the arms aren't underneath the shoulders, and the clubhead can't release. For Mike Wynn, all the parts have to work together so that the clubhead can release itself with the body inside it.

Once, during a lesson, I wanted to start my swing with my arms, hips, and back. My body was outracing my clubhead so that it was always in front of me at impact. My body was creeping into my arms so they couldn't stay away from me. Mike put me on a sidehill and told me to put my weight on my right foot and swing the club, not letting the body get in front of me. Immediately, I noticed my shots were no longer after the fact. My arms under my shoulders were swinging the clubhead again. I noticed that if I was ever going to maintain my height, I had to finish the swing at the same time my weight went over to the left side. My body had to stop diving into my arms. How did Mike know the drill was working for me? Well, first he looked at the face of the club to see if there was a ball mark on the center face. If there were only marks on the toe of the club, then that meant my shoulders were coming over the ball, causing impact after the fact.

Why was I after the fact? Why did my life tend to be after the fact? Because I wasn't a released person. I was still learning by taking divots. I didn't realize yet that divots had no power over me. I wasn't free. But now golf was teaching me that release was here. I was beginning to see that mentors like Mike in a larger,

42

faster, freer world make the game, and life in general, bigger than we are. Release is always in our darkness. Sometimes we get all worked up in golf and in life. We must learn to help each other say, "Release." That way we know the target is already larger inside. The released side of our self which gives you authority now, not later.

A Personal God

Golf taught me that a higher power needs to be personal with us. It's no longer someone else's personal God we must know. It is no longer worrying about the sins of others. It is no longer a map we follow on the golf course that has to go over hazards to get to greens. No, it is a God who is personal, who uses his creation to personally communicate his love to us when we open our hearts to him, to a God who is not otherworldly, but deeper worldly—a God whose love has roots of awareness in his creation for each of us when we realize that everything is from the heart. What we must do is listen to that voice that says, "Sand traps and water have no power over me." We must learn to make the connection between the green and the center face Mike talks about, and learn to connect bridges over troubled waters. The traps don't have to be there, because the bridges over them are more powerful when we open our hearts to the beauty of the course and let the God who communicates with us make that connection. Later, I will say how these connections come from deep roots of awareness that have overcome the world.

Insight

Another thing golf teaches me is that when you are deeper worldly, you know that Jesus has overcome the world. Today it's a world where communication inside the heart learns to see sight from within, or to use what I call "insight." Mike teaches you insight when you get a lesson from him. When my shoulders were going over the top, Mike said I was afraid to turn left because I thought turning left was what caused me to pull the ball. Paradoxically, in golf, the more you spin left, the more the clubface goes out to the target, putting the ball marks on the center face. What Mike saw in my swing was that, because I was fighting to keep my shots from going left, I stopped turning and slid my body to the target. This act of swaying and not turning to the target caused me to let my body get in front of me at impact. This blocking action kept me from releasing the clubhead upward and around. It kept the parts of the swing from waking up inside me because I was swinging after the fact. Swinging after the fact and living after the fact, I was beginning to see the thorn that kept me from releasing the club.

Could Mike Wynn be a so-called bridge over troubled water that could see my swing without a thorn in the flesh inside it, or was I doomed to live in a glass darkly, never to be released? Would I ever see the light at the end of the tunnel before I died, so that I wouldn't live my life after the fact? Golf showed me that if I swung the club after the fact, I was already out of control. I was already dead. So how did Mike get me out of the glass darkly? Well, for one thing, he never worried about the errors I was making in my swing. He just corrected them in the light that was being given to him, to be a professional teacher of golf. Mike said that when you feel the swing, you can't experience release. Release is a knowing in the golfer's heart. You don't just swing the club wildly from the heart. That would put the ball everywhere except where it should be: on the fairway. But you can't overanalyze either. That keeps you in the way of a game that is larger than you are. For Mike, you can't release unless you are awake in your heart.

Awake in the Heart

And what does it mean to be awake in your heart? It is knowing that bad shots happen. They are merely voices inside your head that are trying to disrupt your heart. Peace in golf doesn't come from inside your head. Peace in golf comes when you are patient inside your heart, where good shots are always happening. Golf has taught me that bad shots are merely negative voices. Good shots are reality and will come from the heart if your head doesn't get in the way by keeping you in a glass darkly or inside an ego. Remember, the game of golf is about trusting the sweet spot to always make the connection to the glass lightly. When you don't anticipate bridges, you stay locked up in troubled water. Golf teaches you that there is a communication so the game can speak to you in a way that has ended all doubt. Faith will be added to your swing so that your trust can pass over the troubled waters. Mike would say that "believing gets you there," that it gets you in the hole.

After I receive a lesson from Mike, it always seems there is a shot that says there is a communication on the golf course that I know could only be the voice of Mike Wynn. For Mike, the voice is like the wind. When you swing the club properly, Mike says you can hear the wind of the clubhead releasing. Once you hear the wind, you can trust that your swing is in the zone. You begin to become aware of a *mirror* living inside you and around you. The mirror is the zone. The inside and outside are one. It's no longer only a reward on the inside so that outside doesn't matter. Both matter, because that's what shatters the darkness and enables you to hear the voice that keeps connection inside and outside. The voice is your released side of self.

In the modern world, golf teaches you that the world no longer has to be a map of good and evil. Maps simply can't control a larger, faster, freer universe. We need to become aware of who we are, living inside a mirror, and how—inside that mirror—there could be a golf course where faith and believing in the mirror can end the negative voice that says, "I can't." In the older worldview, maps of good and evil that were defined by the intellect kept people inside a glass darkly while they were on earth. The universe wasn't about the truth of each person.

What golf teaches me is that, unless I believe in the mirror, I can never feel myself being reconstructed by the grace of God breaking the power of evil inside myself.

You can never believe in a zero-tolerant self in Christ. Rather than listening to the glass lightly inside the mirror, you keep letting the map of the course, with all its hazards, be your voice. But suppose the mirror of the course inside you is meant to release you, meant to reconstruct you? If that's true, it should be possible never to have to worry about repeating the mistakes of the past. If you did, you would still be basing your actions on the glass darkly and would not be playing golf inside the mirror, where your bad shots have no power over you. There are still bad shots, but they only happen as part of accepting the emptying out that produces the commitment to good shots.

Open to Mirror

When you learn from Mike Wynn, you start with your own notes. Mike is in your mirror, but it's your mirror. Mike shows you how to own your swing.

Whenever a negative situation presents itself on the course, don't let it put you on an "I can't" map. Learn to stay open to the mirror, which the negative voice inside you can never touch because there are no negative voices inside the mirror. The mirror is your zero-tolerant self. It is the constantly running water that keeps you from the curse. When you play golf on a map, it's like playing only the holes from the book. David Ledbetter is a map teacher. You see, I believe today that all maps are obsolete, because they keep people in a box and people assume the box can be in control of reality. They cause people to have double-standard selves.

Your zero-tolerant self is the truth God is giving you to gather you into his kingdom. The zero-tolerant self—your focus on the light at the end of the tunnel—cannot be broken. God's love for us can't be broken. We break ourselves, but in him it's all release! Let frustration go! Release!

Golf has taught me that if I play in a box, I can never stop the negative voices that keep repeating themselves from inside me. They are always there, like demons I have to fight before I can get on the green. Well, suppose inside the mirror there are no demons to fight. There will still be adversity, but evil will no longer repeat itself so that it puts me on a map. No, the mirror with golf inside it will repeat itself, and we will learn that in God's image creation is good. We will learn that creation is a mirror and that God's image is inside the mirror.

Golf has taught me that I don't have to accept the map from anyone. No one is on a map. We are all inside a mirror of grace. When adversity strikes, don't resort to a map where your dreams that give glory to God will be stopped. Let life inside the mirror correct your sins. You will know they are corrected, because the mirror will speak to you in a way that God makes personal. As long as you continue to make your shots on a map, the negative voice inside the heart of the map will destroy you. Learn to understand your mistakes as a way for you to empty yourself out, until you see the birdies. As you believe more, you will be more committed. You will start to believe the power of evil is broken.

Believe in Positive Voice

To play golf, you must believe release is always present. The negative voice, if you have faith, has been stopped if you accept the negative as emptying out for the love of God. There will still be problems, but now they will always be in a glass lightly so you won't always end up being defined on a map that never ends the glass darkly.

Could golf be the sign that God was sending me, and would I have the courage to step out of the box? What will it take to open the heart of modern man so that he can ignore living inside the glass darkly and believe that the works of the Father are redeeming him? When I myself lived out of the glass darkly, I could never trust the wind. As long as my past repeated itself, I could never play my game inside the mirror where there are no bad shots. Adversity could never be a voice grace could conquer. Adversity would always keep me on a map where my game could never change. I would never have the faith inside me, which could reveal the mirror as I played the course. The map would always be getting in the way. How long could my game, and my life, let the map that couldn't change me take me down with it?

"Mike Wynn's Release with his friends,"
Charlie Laniak, Tom Niles and Bart Steib

What Golf Has Taught Me

At some point you have to jump. You have to believe in what you've been taught. You have to let your faith in a God who is personal, even on the golf course, save you. You have to trust that the mirror will send the game to you if you believe inside the mirror. We have a choice. We can believe in our dreams that are meant to give glory to God, or we can let the map give glory to God by giving up our dreams.

Another thing golf has taught me is that you don't have to give up your dreams. Whenever I do that on the course, or when I buy equipment I think will conquer a perceived problem, I find the negative voice gets stronger. I start worrying about everyone else's sins except my own, and that darkened view on the course keeps repeating bad shots. Instead of being a new person in Jesus, reconstructing myself by the events that occur inside the mirror, I end up letting the negative separate me from the mirror and begin to be destroyed by my lack of confidence. To end the negative voice, golf has taught me that I cannot be afraid of what's out there because I make the same mistakes again and again. When I make the world an enemy, I do the same thing on the course. I give power to the enemy, and divots have power over me.

If it weren't for golf in my life, I would be going down. But God has shown me how golf can be part of his communication, which is telling me that I'm not going down. How does that happen? It happens precisely because the works of the Father inside us will never let us go down unless it's our choice. Why do people want to go down, to fail? Is it because we must go down in this world before we can get to heaven? Is that why we worry about where the ball is going after impact? Is that the hit impulse which makes you stop your swing so you can't follow-through? Suppose golf teaches you that you don't have to go down with the ship to get to heaven. Yes, the game is bigger than we are, but suppose the greatness of the game is that it never lets you go down once you learn the meaning of release. I'm convinced that the pros have learned how good shots repeat themselves in a round of golf when you learn to trust in the mirror which has only good shots inside it. This trust means that the game, like everything in the modern world, comes out of the heart.

What I've learned on the course is that if you don't open your heart to the mirror, the hazards and traps on the course will always end up blocking what your heart is trying to accomplish. Your heart of darkness will keep bringing your goals in life down because you didn't see your goals coming from a heart that is inside your mirror, reconstructing your every moment, when you put faith in your heart and learn to let the mirror be your swing. When the mirror is your swing, the club can release on its own because there is nothing bringing you down getting in the way.

Hearing the Wind

It is interesting to me that when you release the club properly, Mike says, you can hear the wind of the clubhead releasing. Once you hear the wind, you can trust your swing is in the zone. Once you get into the flow or comfort zone, you will understand how release melts the mechanics in your mind that keep the inner knowing from inside the mirror from happening.

Is it possible, in this "wind," to transfer the comfort zone in golf to relaxation with God? Certainly golf is teaching me that religion can become my thorn in the flesh if it's always bringing me down before I die. What we should see is that golf can be part of a world that God has made in his image if you don't let it add power to the glass darkly on the course.

Mike says the game is always bigger than you are, so it becomes dangerous if you think you can ever beat the game. When that happens, the game can mysteriously become your thorn in the flesh. Simply put, the game, like the modern world, is from the heart. The problem is that the heart wants to bring you down. But suppose golf is part of a communication with God from the beginning, which is saying the game of golf doesn't want to bring you down. It is a gift from God to keep you from going down. Golf can be a vehicle from God to give your heart an escape.

The Promised Land

You can never make a positive club selection or make a positive shot if you keep adding power to your divots. All my life, I have wondered where I got the abusive attitude I have toward myself. Is it possible to break this cycle of death within myself, which had become my personal glass darkly? What is the source of the problem? How could the mirror correct my mistakes if I had to always be going down with the ship before I could believe in the mirror? Well, I was beginning to understand that an eighteen-hole round of golf is like a journey to the promised land.

There are traps and hazards along the way, but there are always pars and birdies happening during the round that tell you the game isn't about the power bad shots have over you. That is, of course, if you have faith that there is a light at the end of the tunnel. Well, why wouldn't you have faith? Why did I let the repetition of my bogeys always get in the way of getting to the promised land? Why couldn't I see that pars and birdies reconstructed my past, so that in the future I would know I was going to the promised land, no matter what happened?

You see, in golf, as long as you repeat the cycle of death, you can't see the light at the end of the tunnel. You can't know you are already in the promised land before you die. What golf taught me is that the cycle of death inside you can be broken before you reach the eighteenth hole. Death doesn't have to have the last word. The game can keep you from going down with the ship before you finish your round.

Before I played golf, I had never known a heart that had a tendency toward good inside it before you die. For me, this kind of heart was only given to you if you were proven worthy to receive it after death, when you were judged by God. The problem with that scenario in my life was that I was always adding power to my negative thoughts. Grace could never be in my heart before I died so that my journey to the promised land could begin. Now, golf taught me that the journey could begin before you die. Birdies and pars can happen before you finish the round, even while you are making bogeys. In fact, you might even conclude that the journey is over once you believe. There will still be the emptying, but it won't be a curse. At the same time, golf won't be without emptying out. If it is, you will discover that you will always be in your own way until you accept the emptying out that connects you to being on the course. How sour can you get on yourself? It's all about you, but how much pain is pain enough?

The idea is to never give up on the game. When you get that kind of attitude in a new heart, the game won't let you down before the end of the round. How important it is, I was beginning to see, to have that kind of attitude if you are ever going to break the cycle of death inside yourself. From now on I know that going into bunkers is part of life, but having glimpses of the promised land is also part of life, and those glimpses can be the world connecting you to your roots before death. Why hadn't I seen this before in my life? Why did it take golf to teach me? How could golf connect me to my roots? What were my roots?

For years, I had been taught that my roots were in heaven, an eternity that was separated from life on earth. We were on a journey to another world on earth, and until we died and went to heaven, we would always experience our journey on earth as going down with the ship. Due to original sin, man was born with a tendency toward evil inside his nature. How could I ever play golf with a cycle of death like that inside me? The truth is, I couldn't. But why could Mike Wynn play so well, so released? He was also in the same world, but he didn't play with a cycle of death inside him. He didn't worry about repeating his bad shots. Why did I worry and end up repeating them? How was I ever going to be released from this cycle of death in my heart, causing me to go down with the ship?

Golf taught me that golf could be part of that world being connected to my roots. Golf could have eternity inside it because golf, like life, is not separate from eternity. The attitude you have in golf will be heaven releasing you. In fact, I was learning that golf could even be a grace inside my heart before I die. I mean, why did the game seem not to let me go down? Why did it portray itself to me as a journey inside the promised land before I die? Why did it break the cycle of death inside me even while I was letting my failures beat me up on the course? Wasn't life about adding power to the negative, because it would only be in heaven where the cycle of death would stop? I would have to die before my heart would receive grace. Golf was giving me that grace now and I couldn't explain it.

What I could explain is that maybe the journey doesn't have to all be a valley of tears before you can gain your reward in heaven. Maybe the journey ends in faith once you believe the power of evil is off. You only need the right attitude. But what was that attitude, and how was I learning that attitude from golf? I knew I liked playing golf well, and unless I changed my thinking, I wouldn't play the game well.

I was beginning to see that I needed a new heart, one that didn't separate eternity from life itself—one where the world with golf inside it could be connected to my roots. I started to change my heart because I wanted to play golf well. Golf showed me there was a promised land being revealed to me that seemed to have my eternity inside it, because I knew when I played well that I wasn't taking divots to learn. Everything else in my life seemed to have within it that heart of darkness that couldn't tell me my divots had no power. But golf didn't. Golf was keeping me from going down with the ship. Golf was giving me a glimpse of the promised land before I died. Golf seemed to be a grace in my heart that was keeping me from destroying myself before I die. Golf was keeping me from being annihilated, because at death, I would have already gone down. I wouldn't have glimpsed the promised land before I died.

Now, how could golf give me that glimpse if it was separated from eternity? Suppose it isn't separated from eternity. Suppose it has been restored as a work of the Father by his son. Suppose the spirit uses golf as part of the truth God is using to win my heart. Is it possible that God is happiest when his children are at play? In the modern world, neither external authority nor freedom make you bigger than the game. The larger, faster, freer universe takes the focus off of the self. We are losing ourselves. It's up to us to let God into our hearts so we can find ourselves on the other side now, not later. His authority on the inside and the outside gives us a game to play. Our playing is our freedom in his authority.

An Abusive Worldview

As I reflect on the game of golf in the larger, faster, freer world, the game will always be bigger than I. The universe today is larger than me. I am learning that golf is a game that, like everything else, comes from the heart. But the heart needs to have roots. Where do these roots originate in the heart? For years I always had a heart that would beat itself up. I lived with an abusive view of the world. (Actually, prior to the '60s, people accepted abuse in the world as a way to get into heaven.) Jesus said that all darkness is in the human heart of man. Dying to self by believing only in inner reward won't work in golf. Birdies and enjoying golf are one. The oneness of outside and inside shatters abuse! That's the other side we are drawn to. I learned that you need to fight your way into heaven while you are on earth.

After World War II, one hundred 100-megaton bombs were exploded by Russia and the United States in the air, on land, and in the oceans. Religions were either apocalyptic or earthly, needing to go through death to get to heaven. Beginning in the 1960s, young people began to see that, if you waited until death to be redeemed, it would already be too late, because you would never have stopped the abuse before you died. The problem was that the world was getting larger, faster, and freer. People began to realize that an abusive larger, faster, freer world is already dead—unless you could have a nonabusive heart in the world.

To have a nonabusive heart, you need grace inside you before you die so that death and abuse are no longer inside the heart. How could you ever receive that grace if you had to go through death before it could be there for you? The grace would always be after the fact. Worse yet, in a larger, faster, freer world defined by abuse, we would all be dead. Living outside of the kingdom of Jesus is like living in a home without windows.

Initiating an Interest in Golf

During the 1960s, I was in my twenties. I had joined the ROTC and was an officer in the Army. The Army at that time was not yet a volunteer force. The military too motivated its troops by abuse. Arnold Palmer was just getting started, winning the first of his four Masters titles, and I was beginning to play golf. Being stationed at Fort Ord, California, offered me a great opportunity to play because nearby Monterey has a variety of great courses. Naturally, when I started playing, I had a negative heart on the course. I whined, swore, and threw clubs. I did everything to beat a game you can never defeat. As Mike Wynn says, the game—like the universe—will always be bigger than you are. It must be played from the heart.

But what if my heart is negative? Could my mind keep fighting itself around the golf course because it wasn't influenced by a greater heart? I learned that birdies go along with the inner reward of playing. I needed them to shatter my tendency toward evil. Heaven is the other side now releasing us. Heaven is the released side of ourselves now!

Well, I discovered that, in spite of my tendency toward evil, the game of golf would sometimes reward me, even encourage me so that I wouldn't give up. Then I would wonder why it happened. Well, it seemed to happen in epiphanies. The game seemed to come together for me in a way that didn't let me defeat myself. In fact, the more my wounded heart changed, the better the game responded to me.

It was almost like coming from inside a larger heart in creation, a heart that—when it connected me to being—never left me alone in the universe. Of course, there was still always the danger that my game could come out of a selfish heart in which I felt I could control the game. But every time that happened—every time I let my success come out of my heart and go to my head—I would start grabbing the club and my heart of darkness would surprise me with bogeys and double bogeys. I found myself unable to turn the darkness around, which only led to more bad shots.

Golf, in other words, seemed to have a life of its own, and my heart, be it good or evil, was inside it. If I needed to go through death to eternity in my life, my heart of darkness would always have to go over traps and hazards. If I had a selfish heart on the course, as I said earlier, bad shots would jump out and surprise me. The trick I was beginning to see was how to find the right kind of heart, where good shots were already being created. Could I find that kind of heart on the golf course? Could I see the water running, even as I was emptying out, so life wouldn't be a curse? I believed I could overcome the problem of death inside my nature.

Golf Is a Grace That Wins My Heart

For the first time, golf was teaching me why Jesus had to come to earth. He came to end the problem of death, which curses humanity. He came to end death forever because after the fall man on earth was already dead, unless somehow the works of the Father could be restored to him before he died. Golf was becoming a work of the Father in the roots of Jesus, which would shatter the darkness in my heart before I die. In fact, the more I opened my heart to a new heart, the more I could sense the world around me being connected to the roots of the Sacred Heart of Jesus, which had no death inside it. I was still emptying out, but I was no longer cursed.

Actually, golf was becoming a grace in my new heart, which told me I would live forever. No longer going through death to eternity, I became able to see Jesus and the works of the Father inside him using golf to save me from myself. God was using golf to give my heart an out so I could end the fighting inside myself. Having done away with death, I could now see Jesus on the cross with eternity inside him. And what was that eternity? The eternity was Jesus reaching out his hands for all time to keep us from destroying others. For the first time, I didn't have to win a spiritual battle to get into eternity. Jesus was emptying all the abuse, so now all I had to do was respond to the eternity inside Jesus—which has its roots in the works of the Father—and learn to live my life with a new heart that could open up new avenues for growth in the roots of Jesus. God, in other words, was using golf to empty out my mean spirit.

Golf has taught me that Jesus Christ is eternity. Outside of him, either in a glass darkly or in a selfish heart, I was beginning to understand that my life would only be about being cursed or hopeless in my own way. Golf teaches me that there is never any excuse for giving into evil. That is why Jesus came: to shatter the darkness that creates the curse. When I had that positive attitude on the golf course, the game seemed to come to me. If I could get that same kind of attitude in my life, maybe life would do the same. I was beginning to understand and adapt the maxim in the movie *Field of Dreams,* which says, "If you build it, he will come." I also was learning to have my pain erased in my new confidence and was beginning to think about going the distance—not the distance to heaven, but the distance I needed to go to live a fulfilling life.

I was beginning to see that if you accept Jesus as your Lord and savior, you will live together in his roots, which reach out forever to keep people from going down. Because these roots have no death inside them, and because I am inside these roots by faith, I must live forever right now. The tendency toward evil is no longer in those roots because those roots are no longer taking you to heaven through death. My roots are not in heaven. They are now in Jesus Christ, who brings heaven to earth inside the roots he gets from the works of the Father at the beginning of time, and through his death on the cross, which ended the curse for all time.

Another thing golf teaches you is that the roots of the Father have unintended purposes inside them. For example, I've been going to Centreville Golf Center for years to buy clubs. Centreville Golf is owned by Mr. Choi and is located in Centreville, Virginia. One Sunday, I was looking for a putter and stopped by to talk to Mr. Choi. It just so happened that a Japanese pro, who called himself Jim, was at the shop. I asked him to look at my swing because I was having trouble sucking the club inside on my back swing, and not swinging the club into the air. "Why," I asked him, "does this event keep happening?" He said that the clubface is always pointed to the target, something like Mike Wynn had always told me. "Well," Jim said, "when you start your swing, keep the clubface pointed to the target and swing it upward at the moment it moves away from the target." It was just as Mike Wynn says: "Set your hands in the swing motion so you aren't too mechanical, keeping the clubface pointing to the target." In Mike's perception, if you are soft in your elbows during the takeaway, the clubface will always point to the target, and that happens when the takeaway is in a swing motion. Meeting Jim made a connection to Mike Wynn.

A Compassionate Universe

We are always learning in the modern world, sometimes in an unintended way. In a larger, faster, freer universe, everything learned comes from the heart without abuse inside it. Golf has taught me that the universe should be compassionate. We are evolving in a compassionate universe, not an abusive one. God does not base evolution on abuse, as is the case in natural selection. The image of God inside our hearts is without abuse. We evolve in God's image by the way we see our intellect emerging from our dreams, which awaken our hearts in Christ. Golf teaches you to stand strong in a zero-tolerant heart.

Let's face it: If everything we learned was intended by a map of good and evil, how would we explain the unintended experiences we have in our lives, as when I met Jim at Mr. Choi's golf shop? We can't, but unexpected occurrences must happen, or we couldn't grow. We would either end up in a glass darkly, or we would only understand abuse as the prime motivating factor in evolution and end up with selfish hearts. Golf defines our destiny, because golf is played in a compassionate, evolving universe. Golf has its roots in the works of the Father, which are our dreams revealed to us in our sacred hearts without neglect. Today, God reveals his dreams to us. Golf teaches you to never give in to abuse of any kind on the course. When you learn to be a soldier on the course, you will soon see eternity in Jesus without abuse communicating a friendly universe to you, not an abusive one. You will learn to be, and allow your heart without abuse to open to your dreams.

At this point, one may ask whether it is necessary to know you have an abusive heart before you can change it. We learn from golf that, unless you admit you are feeling something from inside your heart, you can never master the game. It seems, as St. Paul says, that admitting you are fighting something does not mean there isn't a light at the end of the tunnel. It just means we are on a journey that is defined by the unintended roots in our lives, which goes back to the works of the Father, restored by eternity in Jesus Christ for all of us now.

The game of golf is a journey out of darkness until you believe the roots of the Father inside Jesus has saved you. But once you believe, the journey is over. It doesn't have to begin at death. That would be too late, after the fact. It can begin immediately when you open your heart to a greater heart that doesn't want to see you in a glass darkly for any reason. Once we accept emptying out, we will begin to see the mirror, which has already corrected our mistakes. Instead of fighting ourselves after bad shots and adding more abuse, we can let the roots of the game of golf inside Jesus correct our mistakes forever. Remember, the journey is over now. The abuse inside us ends immediately when we believe the light is shattering the curse in our hearts. Our hearts need to change because the fear of death has left us alone. We are never alone in the light. We are truly released.

We need to know the love of God in our lives, which,ends all aloneness in Jesus Christ. I found that I could know that love on the golf course. I could see that the course is a mixture of traps and greens, hazards and fairways, and birdies and bogeys. In my abusive heart, it always seemed that I was fighting a glass darkly in the traps and hazards, even though the fairways were always there beckoning me to make good shots. Why couldn't I make those shots? Couldn't I see the light at the end of the tunnel and begin to believe that the mirror on the course had already corrected my mistakes so I could know I was already inside the promised land? Sure, I would still hit the ball in traps, but I was beginning to understand that birdies could still be there before I ended my round. I could be going to the promised land while I was hitting the ball into hazards. In fact, the promised land was already there on the fairways and greens, pulling me out of traps as long as I let belief in the promised land get me in the hole.

A Golfer's Life

A player whom I admired, who I think always saw golf as belief in the promised land, was Arnold Palmer. In his book, _A Golfer's Life_, Arnold wrote about how his father told him to put his hands on the club a particular way. Arnold felt his dad's hands over his own and he said he never lost that impression. His dad's hands were in the promised land, which released Arnold's swing. At Arnold's golf course in Latrobe, Pennsylvania, there is a statue of his dad that overlooks the course. It's all part of the promised land for Arnold.

In fact, _A Golfer's Life_ is about a journey where obstacles never allow one to believe that the promised land is not always there. Arnold has experienced failure in his life, but never has he let his failures get in the way of his go-for-broke attitude. I suspect that Arnie believes the promised land is a thread that continuously runs through his life. He brings this type of faith to the golf course. It is a faith that was passed on to him by his beloved father. This faith never stops believing there is a promised land already there, ready to deliver him.

When Arnie was only eleven years old and not yet a member of the country club in Latrobe, Pennsylvania, he told himself that someday he would own the country club. And you know what? He eventually owned Latrobe Country Club, exactly as he had believed.

Like Mike Wynn, Arnie believes you should never put yourself above the game. He learned this principle from his father. I believe that Arnie has always been able to let his belief in the promised land take him where he was going. That's why he is called "The King" by many. He is, of course, but only so that you might believe in the glory coming out of the roots of his eternity in Jesus.

Often, Arnold will come into a life like a mystical traveler. Once, when I was in Boston at a senior tournament, I found myself under a tent during a rainstorm with Arnold for nearly an hour. He was resplendent in his blue shirt, gray flannel slacks, and dark tan. He was coming out of the promised land, and the promised land was shining through him. Ten years later, at another senior tournament at Hobbit's Glen, Maryland, Arnold made eye contact with me until my eyes needed to turn away. It was as though I had known him, but the promised land coming from inside his being was too much for me, so I had to turn away from his face.

You see, golf teaches that all things he has created are shining, and it's up to us to follow lights like Arnie's and Mike's to the promised land. They are inside the promised land because they believe the promised land is already being made known to them. The king is magnificent because he never apologizes for being a light in the tunnel, but he never uses his greatness to take advantage. He knows it's not about greatness, it's about the promised land, where all of God's people already live in glory. To me, Mike Wynn and Arnie represent the lights already inside the tunnel, until I have the chance to see all things shining.

Basketball

My basketball coach at William & Mary had that quality of being a light already inside the tunnel taking me to the promised land which was already here. When I started on the freshman basketball team in 1963, Joe Agee, our coach, played me the first seven games, even when I was only scoring three or four points a game. I couldn't sleep at night for fear of being benched. But he still played me, until suddenly I ran off a game against Louisburg Junior College in North Carolina in which I scored forty-seven points. It was a school record at that time, but it wouldn't have been possible had I not had a coach who could see me playing basketball in the promised land, so that I could believe that the promised land was always there to keep me from going down with the ship.

In 1963 I had hardly played any golf, but I was already beginning to sense the meaning of a promised land while going through the tunnel. However, golf made me aware that the promised land is what gets you out of the tunnel altogether. Is it possible that the works of the Father restored by Jesus are meant to send us Mike Wynns, Arnie Palmers, and Joe Agees so we can believe that promised land is always with us in the people whom God sends us to keep from going down?

I have a very good friend named Tom Niles, who played basketball with me at William & Mary, and who was a member of the golf team coached by Joe Agee. From the time I knew Tom, I always was going to eternity through death. Tom, on the other hand, never abused himself or beat himself up on the course. Tom, like Joe Agee, had that special quality in the mirror that corrected me by his presence when I decided I didn't want to be wounded. Who was behind my meeting these people? Is it a grace from God before I die so I won't live a cursed life? What seems possible is that a higher power, who already knows our thorns, sends the promised land to us without thorns. These people are meant to inform us that heaven is over us now. Eternity is in Jesus, and death is no more. Otherwise, why do we stop beating ourselves up? Remember, even though I was playing poorly, Coach Agee stayed with me, and I ended up scoring forty-seven points.

Like Mike Wynn and Vijay Singh, we have to trust that the swing in the promised land is already present. Otherwise, why would Mike Wynn help me? Why would Tom Niles stay with me? Why would Joe Agee keep playing me? I did not know the answer at that time. But, foreshadowing my future struggles with golf, I was still fighting the cycle of death inside me. I still hadn't learned how golf as a work of the Father was starting to break my cycle of death, so I could believe the promised land was with me. I was still not released. I was still going to the promised land by annihilating myself before I died and never getting there because I was always too late.

I needed to learn how release was already opening my eyes so that blinking over a big shot would be an accident. I still didn't believe that my good shots in the promised land are that which is real. My bad shots are accidents. I still didn't understand how good shots without blinking were always there in the works of the Father, and my blinks were accidents. I was still connecting my blinks together like a poor history lesson and refused to connect my good shots so I could reconstruct a bad past. Knowing that your good shots are always erasing your bad ones reconstructs your confidence in God's image. Bad shots are accidents. Your good shots are who you are.

Who Am I?

The problem is that I didn't know who I was. Unless golf makes us authentic people, like Arnold Palmer, we will lose perspective playing golf. The good news is I wasn't losing perspective, but I often wondered whether the game replacing the abuse inside me was real. My negative voice kept telling me golf was an illusion: "Don't trust the game. You are being set up to fail."

Once when I was playing, I was totally focused on myself and the game playing inside my heart. I was so alone in myself that by the time I got to the thirteenth hole, I was totally unaware of how others were playing in my group. In fact, unbeknownst to me, a beautiful terrier was following our group. I wasn't totally unaware of the dog; but I certainly didn't make him part of the promised land taking me through the glass darkly. He was a nuisance and not in the big picture. I had been brought up with the tendency toward evil in my nature, so, the dog, in my mind, was part of the ongoing evil I needed to fight if I was ever going to get to the promised land. I was being taken in by the darkness. I had yet to understand how the promised land already present makes us beautiful hurricanes or perfect storms. Well, the dog knew he was in the promised land.

Suppose the dog, the grass, the tee, and the view of the mountains are all there, and my lack of awareness that all is one is keeping my swing from a deeper realization of the flesh that faith is real. I couldn't see the outside and inside as *one*. I was either all inside meaning or all outside, playing only for trophies. This book is about authority on the inside and outside, which owns the game outside because the game is played on the other side—the released side of self. Authority is a love for the game that focuses you when you are afraid so that you can have freedom in authority. Authority is the released side of golf! I couldn't see myself or the dog or my playing partners because everything was in the box. I was still learning to think out of the box. I was still learning to think in epiphanies, in a larger, faster, freer world filled with abuse. Abuse ends up being the box. To think out of the box, you must open your heart to epiphanies, which affect each one of us in very subjective ways. What we learn one day about life on a golf course might teach us, as it did Arnold Palmer and Mike Wynn, lessons to be learned off the course.

When Jesus took death away, he became eternity without abuse for all of us. Eternity communicates by epiphanies with no abuse inside them. When I asked the question earlier about being set up, I was beginning to see that original sin would always put doubt inside you about who you are. For my whole life, original sin in my nature has been a cycle of abuse I have needed to continually correct if I were ever going to heaven. The problem is that Jesus ended up going through a cycle of abuse to get to heaven. He knew that abuse of this magnitude would be catastrophic two thousand years later unless we could define ourselves by who we really are in God's image and shatter any darkness we perceive in ourselves. Once eternity comes out of Jesus with no abuse inside it, how could you be set up? That would be abuse. Sometimes God doesn't allow us to receive the good because he knows we would abuse it and that abuse would keep blocking the gift.

What I was learning is that until you can let go and believe that everything has no abuse inside it (because Jesus has ended all abuse), you will never understand the meaning of release. Because the tendency toward evil was inside me, because I would keep fighting it all the way to heaven, because I had to go through the hurricane to be beautiful, I was never able to fully release. My release was blocked by the original sin, always inside me and inside everything else. I couldn't stop making the world my enemy.

Can modern man live in a larger, faster, freer world if he keeps projecting abuse onto everything? How much abuse is abuse enough? If you define yourself by darkness inside you, you never see the law in the communication with God, which says you can believe you are already in God's image. My perception of abuse had gotten so bad that when I finally noticed the terrier I'd otherwise been unable to see, it represented a threat to me. I couldn't see the dog in the epiphany meant to raise me from the dead before I die. The heart that I missed surprised me on the thirteenth hole. What do you think happened? On the thirteenth hole, the dog saw four golf bags lying on the fairway. Amazingly, he walked over to my bag in the middle of the pack, stepped over it, and pissed all over my bag, completely ruining it. How did he know which bag was mine? How did he know I was in the glass darkly? When the other guys heard and saw the story, they broke out in uncontrollable laughter. It's still a story repeated in the locker room at Evergreen Country Club. But the incident told me that dogs know who is in the promised land.

Laws and rules aren't about controlling original sin inside your nature, I was learning. No, morality has to do with being a better person. It is never because you have original sin inside you. What you have is a voice trying to get you to listen to abuse, and not open to the eternity all around you in Jesus ending the abuse when you totally trust in God. The trick is to believe Jesus is the root of our eternity and has already opened the gates to the promised land so that we can be saved in a reality with no abuse.

As long as I had that darkness inside me, the dog would keep getting in the way of my confidence, when it's really the original sin that I have imagined in myself. This is the price of Adam's sin, but his sin is not who we are. We are the person we become when we open our hearts to Jesus and allow him to drink the poison inside us by his death on the cross. Once we accept that we are fighting something and allow him to drink the poison, we are set free by the sacrifice of his blood. The poison leaves us and moves to his body when we accept how he is emptying us out. Until we believe there is no poison in redeemed creation, we will keep abusing the spirit that God gives us every moment in creation.

In golf, his spirit is the belief that the birdies have already ended the abuse, which is the traps and hazards on the course. Rather than going through the storm to the greens, it's very important to turn the golf course into a beautiful darkness—beautiful, because the beauty of golf already ends the abuse, which are the traps, hazards, and bad swings. To play well, you must learn to let belief get you in the hole.

Talking with Another Champion

Recently, I took a golfing vacation to Wisp Resort in Deep Creek, West Virginia. While there, I had the opportunity to speak to the two-time national long-driving champion, Scott DeCandia. I mentioned to Scott that I kept having the problem of pulling the club inside on the downswing. I couldn't get my arms away from my body. Scott said I was locking my left shoulder on the downswing, that when I locked my shoulder, the butt handle of the club would come into my body. I told Scott about how Mike Wynn said I was stopping the club after impact and not finishing the swing. Whatever it was, I couldn't stop putting the butt end of the club into my body. So I asked Scott DeCandia how one can play this game when there are so many blocks that keep one from having epiphanies. Scott answered my question exactly as Mike Wynn did. He said the game will reward you if you accept it as a game that is continually breaking you down. In other words, you play the game of golf from your heart. The game will only make its peace with you when you never give up on the perfect dream inside your heart. For Scott DeCandia, the perfect dream was being the long drive champion. For Mike Wynn, the perfect dream is the golf swing itself. Sure, along the way the game will break you down, but you must let the promised land take you through the rough waters until your dream becomes reality. Reality is the authority. God gave it to these men that had their ownership inside it. We must own the game of life too. Reality is knowing the released side of yourself.

Dreams Can Become Reality

Golf has taught me that dreams can become a reality even while life is breaking you down. And I have also learned that a round such as the one I had in Williamstown can be a beautiful hurricane. The true golfer is a perfect warrior. You keep moving on the course during your round and never give up on the possibility of a perfect score. Original sin on the course will try to take your dream from you, but you can never give in to that voice or you will never get out of the hazards around the course. You will keep beating yourself up and will never see the beauty of your round without abuse. You must have deep faith in the beauty of the works of the Father by staying open to how the greatness of the game is opening to you with no abuse.

The game not only will affirm your being, but the whole idea of being present to you without abuse will be reinforced inside you. Imagine my feelings when I began to see a world without abuse. My whole world began to open up as friendly and compassionate in the midst of adversity. We are all called to be beautiful hurricanes by our faith. Yes, God can use golf as he uses freedom—to gather us into his authority. When we play with his authority, we are free. We learn to own our games from his love for us!

But what about that problem with my left shoulder locking up and keeping my swing in a box of abuse? How could the dream or the swing in the promised land end this abuse?

I returned to Mike Wynn and asked him about the left shoulder stopping my club and causing me to pull inside. Mike, as is his fashion, immediately said, "You're not locking up your left shoulder. You are locking everything up. You're forgetting about being soft, and that is leaving your hands behind you and locking your shoulders." Mike said I had to unlock everything. There are no individual parts to your movement when you swing from start to finish without any tension. Swinging freely is release because nothing separates you from what is waking up from inside your heart. Original sin tries to separate you, to break you down, but your belief that the swing without abuse is present eventually saves you. The light shatters the darkness, which is why you are able to accept emptying out as the condition for believing the water always runs. Original sin will try to distract you, but your authentic self will always show you your next shot.

Once you get the softness, Mike says, there are no positions. The swing happens because it's natural for the club to be where it's supposed to go when you don't put it into position. But why did I force the club into position? I know that I am fighting something, but I can't get my swing out of the box. "Why," I asked Mike, "after all of your lessons, am I still pulling the shaft inside my body?" Mike said, rather bluntly, "You have to trust your swing, but before you can do that, you need to trust, period. Let go. The swing from inside your heart is already there, but you don't believe it." Mike says you have to experience a kind of knowing even when you can't see it happening. It's a sense of footsteps walking alongside while you are breaking down. It's a sense of trust revealing to you the light inside the swing, even when you don't feel it. What is the light, this knowing? It's the notes from being winning your heart, and golf is in the trust when you accept the emptying out.

The Swing

Slowly, I was beginning to understand how the swing is a motion you try to perfect yet you can't feel. I couldn't feel it because the image of the perfect swing cannot arise from inside my being unless I allow it to be a gift. The swing has to win my heart. You can never allow it to be a gift when you always put the club in position. When you do that you are not acknowledging a higher being behind the swing with you inside it. Can this higher being answer my questions of pulling the club into my body? How was I to trust the clubhead already being in position? Mike said I had to stop locking up my body in the clubhead. He said this affected how the clubhead would finish the swing. I said that I needed to start the swing with everything in the clubhead. "Well," Mike said, "I don't care how free your body is in the clubhead. It's still waggling at the top, which means to me you are separating the parts. And when you separate the parts, you are going through self-abuse to get to the finish. As long as you go through self-abuse, the parts will always be separated, and the lack of softness will continue to put the club in the wrong position when the right position is already there with no abuse inside it."

When a released person swings the golf club, there is no separation; there is only the freedom of all the parts working together independently. But what about starting the swing? I asked Mike how he started the swing. He said the power to start the swing comes from inside—the awareness of the motion of the body in space. Mike said that power to start the swing is derived from an awareness that all the parts in the swing are in motion when you feel soft in your arms at address. The awareness at address that the whole swing finishes in the motion of the body makes you soft. Rigidity at address restricts motion and keeps the club in the wrong position throughout the swing. Mike said that when I didn't let my arms hang freely, I would get much too mechanical. He wanted my arms to hang freely all the way to the finish, not just at address. Mike said that the swing had to be totally in sync with the motion of the body—a natural consequence of letting my arms hang free. He reminded me that the start of the swing is a motion I can't feel yet am always trying to perfect.

In one lesson, I couldn't stop throwing the club behind me. I asked Mike why I still had this problem; clearly, I was extremely frustrated. Mike said the problem was still there because I lack trust. He said that every time he corrects me, I put his teaching into my head and become too mechanical. It's not about mechanics, Mike said. He teaches people to recognize mistakes in their swings, which, if they avoid, will enable the swing just to happen.

Mike is after tempo. His lessons show that as long as you are mechanical, your swing will never have the proper tempo. He once noticed that I kept stopping my follow-through. I asked Mike what he wanted me to do so I wouldn't stop the club after impact. He said, "There you go again. Don't look for a reason why you stop the club. Just don't stop the club, and the swing will finish on its own. Don't get in the way of what the clubhead already wants to do." He told me to just let the swing be, because being in my swing has always been there since the beginning of creation. Through this new understanding, golf began to reveal myself to me as a person who was fighting who I already was in God's image. Just like my stuttered swing, I couldn't let *God's* image happen without always getting in my own way. Mike showed me how I was getting in my own way, and I began to look for the explanation for how to swing the club rather than just swinging it without purpose. I had become a slave to my mind, and my mind was cloning my swing. My swing lacked the presence of the notes from being inside my heart and the phenomena surrounding me. But why did I overanalyze?

I asked Mike whether he remembered the gospel story of Thomas putting his hands into the flesh of Jesus after he had risen from the dead. Mike said he did, so I asked him if Jesus wanted Thomas to believe that Jesus was risen or to believe that in him our flesh is real. In other words, is my faith only about the Lord being risen and not about my flesh being more real, as eternity from the risen Jesus ends the abuse inside me? The problem, Mike was telling me, is that I had a self and because I didn't acknowledge it, I was locking my body and the clubhead up, thus preventing what already had happened in the works of the Father from finishing my swing with me inside it. For Mike, freedom in the swing meant all the parts working together independently and in sync. The spirit behind the phenomena of the swing is one with the Father, and the Father who is totally free is one with all the phenomena who feel his pleasure.

For the first time, I was beginning to see how separated I was from the freedom I needed to have if ever I was going to swing the clubhead without my old nature inside it. I was beginning to understand from my lessons with Mike how Jesus was telling Thomas that, inside Jesus, your flesh becomes more real because the universe is one with the freedom inside the works of the Father, who has created everything in his image. In golf, Mike said that any separation would prevent the clubhead and the body from working as one, thus keeping the golfer from ever enjoying the pleasure of the Father, whose free gift of his oration is responsible for this game.

Faith

Golf was now teaching me that true faith is reality, becoming more real all the way into eternity. In the golf swing, faith means the flesh becomes more real the more the body is inside the clubhead and the clubhead is inside the body. Faith means that our lives become more real inside Christ, and Jesus becomes more real inside us. All people are one inside the freedom of the Father enjoying his pleasure, and the Father is inside all people who have a heart that can't say no to God's image of love inside them. Just as in golf, as long as the clubhead is separated from the body, we have seen how the parts can't be in sync. When that happens, there is no freedom present that can release the spirit and image of our creator inside us. Now, when I play golf, I want to release my swing because then I know I am living for the glory of God. I know he is being, revealing to me his notes.

Breaking Down

Each year the group of guys who play golf with me at Evergreen Country Club in Haymarket, Virginia, make a three-day trip to play golf. One year we went to the famous Cascades course in Hot Springs, Virginia. We would always call the Cascades course the "Hots" because it was really easy to get lathered up when you played that course.

One particular round, I had a chance to break 80 for the first time at the Hots. I needed only three bogeys with only three holes to play. Well, on the sixteenth hole, a par 5, I hit my ball into the water on my third shot and ended up with a seven. On the next par 5, the seventeenth hole, I tried to hook my second shot around the comer and ended up pushing the ball to the right into the creek. I got another seven. Then, on the par 3 eighteenth hole, I dumped my first shot into the water and ended up with a five. Six over par for my last three holes for a round of 83!

I didn't know, as I do now, that the game of golf, which was breaking me down, was a light at the end of the tunnel. I had a cross in my nature and could never see the light of a new nature in God's image transforming my old nature. Abuse was in my nature and it showed up when all the guys went out to a steakhouse for dinner. While there, I was still feeling the Hots and when my friend John Anderson began to josh me. I waved my fork in the air and told this large 250-pound former Memphis State tackle that if he didn't keep quiet, I'd come to where he was sitting and stick him with my fork. I am only 170 pounds. It was really funny to the guys because everyone knew "Big John" could snap me like a twig. Yet I was taking it all seriously. I couldn't see all the breaking down as the light coming toward me from the end of the tunnel. I clearly was not released and could not enjoy a steak dinner. The Hots had made me delirious. I was blind to the light that shatters the darkness.

Mike Wynn had told me that on the course the pros experience the same breaking down, but always coming toward them from the end of the tunnel. Why did I not see the light coming toward me? Because at that time in my life, I could not understand that life is a journey into epiphanies. It's the leap of faith in

Jesus Christ that has to be there if we are ever going to get the cross out of our natures and believe that we are already released by the works of the Father.

You see, when Jesus came to earth, he died for us so we could see each day as a journey into a released life. What we have to learn to do is not to use our natures as excuses for not living released lives. From now on, when you miss putts, it's no longer in your nature. The cross is a negative voice that tries to stop the light from coming toward you from the end of the tunnel. The glass darkly is the larger, faster, and freer universe that doesn't give you any attention—no focus. Golf is a glass lightly, releasing the pressure of the glass darkly. Life without Christ is a glass darkly. With Jesus, life can be a light with golf inside it on the other side, now shattering the glass darkly.

Golf has taught me that I am no longer going to the light in a nature with traps and hazards inside it. No, the fairways and greens always come toward me from the end of the tunnel. I still miss putts, but I know now that missed putts aren't in my nature, because the light correcting those shots is always coming to me. I've learned to trust that the journey around a golf course is more about the light coming toward me than it is about the abuse inside me. The abuse is still there, but now golf has taught me it's only a voice, and that rather than fight the voice in a spiritual battle, I accept the voice as an emptying out of the darkness in my nature and learn to trust the water always running in the emptying out, until I know the light is always present. What is real is the light with my authentic self always coming toward me from the end of the tunnel. What is real is learning to flow with the Father.

The Flow

Once you and I begin to imagine we are inside a new nature in God's image, we will begin to trust more in the light coming toward us than we will in the abuse inside us that we think we have to correct. Just let the abuse be a voice emptying you out, and let your new nature be what is real. I know this is very controversial because some Christians stay on the cross, doing time all throughout their lives on earth. I say there are crosses, but they are always inside the darkness. There is light. Let release, not the cross without Christ, save you! The cross without Christ is a glass darkly. The cross with Christ is the released side of self!

This fits most definitely into Mike Wynn's definition of the swing as a kind of magic realism. You can't feel the swing, because there is no secret to it. It's who you are in the works of the Father, from the beginning of creation. The remembrance of the beginning of creation restored by Jesus Christ is a journey each moment into release, until there are no longer any negative voices. Once we gain confidence that golf can be notes from being inside the mirror, we can begin to trust that God is breaking into our world and transforming it into a state of grace. Does this mean we don't have to fight wars? Of course not. But now fighting wars is because we are being emptied. But why let war empty us? We can empty on the golf course and keep the state of grace alive that is in the world.

Dismiss the Negative Voice

For centuries before us, and even today in the Middle East, people wake up wanting to die to reach their dreams. They worry more about what's going to happen to them after they die than they do about wanting to live in the light. Mike said that unless you "break down," you can't be released. It's the light breaking you down from the end of the tunnel that will eventually get you to trust more in the journey into release than in correcting the abuse to be released. For the first time, you will begin to live inside a new nature without abuse inside it, because you won't be able to use your old nature as an excuse. Your old nature is now a voice emptying you out. As Mike said, the reason you have to admit you are fighting something is because this voice doesn't like the person you are becoming. Dismiss the old nature as a negative voice—not who you really are—and not a self you can use as an excuse for all of the crosses in your life. Crosses are no longer curses. They represent the emptying out of your darkness to make room for your salvation.

Once you begin to translate this new nature into golf, you begin to realize that release is all about tempo. *Tempo* is the authority you feel God gives you to own your game so it can be free! We always work for ownership of our lives so that we can gain the authority from God. He uses authority to gather us into his kingdom now! The other side is our release side. We are on the other side now! I believe that God loves tempo, and his greatest pleasure comes when we feel his tempo, not only on the golf course but also in life. Because we are human, we don't always feel his tempo. However, what golf teaches you is to not dwell on the dark side of being human, no matter what happens to you on the golf course. I believe the successful players always believe the power of darkness has already been defeated. For years, I defined my life by correcting the abuse inside my nature. When you play golf, you can't say you miss putts because it's inside your nature not to hit straight putts. When you journey around a golf course with abuse inside you, you can't stop the negative from coming around.

Be Free of Beelzebub

My good friend Jim Clark, a member of Evergreen Country Club in Haymarket, Virginia, always tells me I carry Beelzebub on my shoulder. Jim believes that to be successful in golf you need to play believing your nature is free of Beelzebub. Jim is a gentleman on the course. He never lets Beelzebub get up on his shoulder. Once, he was trying to tell me something about the swing, and I said to Jim that I don't listen to 12 handicaps. That's an example of Beelzebub perched on my shoulder. Well, Jim went out, practiced hard, took a lesson, and bought a new driver, and today, at age fifty-eight, he is one of the finest players in our club. He didn't let my Beelzebub get inside him, and when I play against Jim today, his presence is indomitable. He exudes grace and confidence.

What I'm learning on the golf course is that there is a reality out there without Beelzebub. Instead of defining myself inside Beelzebub as if the abuse is inside me, I am beginning to define the dark side in my humanity as Beelzebub perched on my shoulder. People like Jim, Tom, and Mike teach me that golf is a game that destroys the negative.

It's a game that is played inside in Christ, and in God's image, as long as we stand tall so that Beelzebub can't get inside us. Actually, good tempo results from your ability to play golf without abuse. When you feel Beelzebub, you must believe his power has already been broken and allow your true nature in God's image restored by Jesus Christ to take control of your life.

Power of Evil

On the golf course, the power of evil is symbolized by the traps and hazards. But these negative components are not inside us unless we define who we are by the way we correct abuse in ourselves and don't let ourselves believe that the good from the end of the tunnel has already chased away the negative. Imagine—it took golf to teach me that a power of good is shattering the darkness. I don't have to make every shot a spiritual battle with myself. My struggle is really to believe that being won't pass me by, so I am not afraid.

For centuries, humans have been taught to believe so that they could get the abuse out of their natures. It was necessary to have sin in your nature before you could receive grace. Human nature was an excuse for weakness. People were cowards if they didn't die to the abuse inside them. But suppose there is no abuse inside you. Suppose a coward is someone who refuses to believe that a relationship with Jesus will restore people to their true selves. All of us were born with God's image inside us. As Bagger Vance told Mr. Junuh in the movie *The Legend of Bagger Vance,* "You are a hard man, Mr. Junuh, to think your whole life on earth is spent without any meaning."

We are all born to make life meaningful for one another. We are born to live out our lives in a state of grace. But we also have free will and some people choose to live with Beelzebub on their shoulders. They choose to let being pass them by until life becomes a curse. In golf, like life, however, that's a prescription for disaster. Unless we can see the game in the mirror rejecting Beelzebub on our shoulder, we will always live in the glass darkly and never reach those heights where we know the victory over Satan has already been defeated, and no matter what the circumstances, know that the ball will always roll in the fairway. And even if it doesn't, because our faith says the power of evil has been broken, we can believe that the birdies will keep being there from the end of the tunnel because we believe.

Belief in Self

There are no true repeatable stories on the golf course. The game is about making you believe, making you have faith, until you get the understanding that believing is what will set your game, and your life, in motion. Belief is what gets you around the golf course. What better game is there for the larger, faster, freer world where the mind, trapped inside itself with no heart, will try to perch on the shoulder until the abuse is unbearable? I've seen abuse destroy so many people when they play, myself included. But the good news is that golf doesn't have to be played with abuse. It has to be played with tempo, and tempo can only be there when you don't give in to Beelzebub being perched on your shoulder.

Golf is not a game where you systematically chase away your bad shots. When you do that, you let Beelzebub come up on your shoulder. You might even believe that abuse is inside you. Golf is the light from the end of the tunnel that shows me that it's possible to break the power of the cross inside you. Just change your attitude and let believing in your new heart be the power that chases Beelzebub away. When you learn that tempo, the good shots repeat themselves and the bad shots are the exceptions. But you have to keep believing and allow yourself to be convinced that birdies are greater than bogeys because they are always coming from the end of the tunnel to repel bogeys.

Revisiting Trust

Trust is an idea discussed throughout this book because the authority to play this game is a gift from God on the inside and outside, shattering the darkness. Release is everywhere. Release gives us authority!

As I came to understand after working with Mike Wynn, golf teaches you to trust because it's only by trust that you can get out from underneath the coward's heart. Tiger Woods and Arnold Palmer are players who make every shot a total commitment even before they execute the shot. For them, the logic of the game follows from believing, but it is never the source of belief. For these players, golf is always winning their hearts. In a larger, faster, freer world, golf is a game that teaches you to believe. As long as you look for a true story in the game of golf, your mind won't be strong enough to repel the darkness trying to conquer your heart. Your heart and your trust in the greater glory of God is the only way you can repel the negative that is trying to destroy being. Golf can't be played with a coward's heart, which doesn't believe good things will happen. Golf teaches you that no matter what happens in the game, believing can get you where you will always know that the ball rolling into the fairway or cup is always chasing away the voice that tells you your missed shots are inside you. In a larger, faster, freer world, golf challenges us to think about how much abuse is enough.

So much of our world today is not defined by belief or by a spirit winning our hearts. We have become clones who need to be released from our copied selves. We are "cloned" because we are all trophy heads, bigger than the game or dying to ourselves so that we can have an inner reward for playing. We must see the inside and the outside together, giving us authority from God to free us with birdies. The other side now is the release side of ourselves. It's not about always needing a true story before you believe. It's about not having a coward's heart and allowing belief to take you where you want to go. It's about being totally committed to believing, the way Tiger Woods is totally committed to every shot.

When I played that round of golf at Taconic Golf Club in Williamstown, Massachusetts, it was as though I had a glimpse of heaven. But heaven was not somewhere else. Heaven was breaking from by being as a light from the end of the tunnel. It wasn't about evil being in my nature and getting a glimpse of what heaven is like somewhere else. Not heaven, but that round was the light from the end of the tunnel. It was in me to play that round of golf so that someday I might be convinced that Jesus had broken the cross inside me. We must never let the cross be inside us as a curse, because that would be denying the great works of Jesus. He came so that we would not live with cowardly hearts and so that we could learn to be totally committed to life. Golf has taught me that the ball will indeed roll onto the fairway if you keep believing during your round and accept the emptying out as the path with a light at the end of the tunnel.

The fact of the matter is that the mind on the golf course and in life will never produce a true story. A true story can only be discovered when you believe and allow faith, and trust, to win your heart with the notes that being sends you when you empty out. We should be convinced by believing until we can let it go on the golf course. You will never see the freedom if it's only defined by reason. Freedom can only be in the notes that win your heart. Reason alone is not enough against a heart filled with notes from being. A new nature is revealed by God's image, which is inside you and which overpowers you when faced with the darkness that is trying to reject it.

In the golf swing, I have seen how Mike never wants me to put the club into positions during my swing. In Mike's view, when you are inside your new nature at address, there are no positions. The swing is already in place and the tempo is set. For Mike, it seems that heaven is a kind of state of bliss where you learn to live in the moment. Everything that ever will be has already happened. We just have to get out of God's way so we can see his tempo (or mirror, or state of grace) working in our lives. Crosses will still be there, but no longer are they curses inside you. They are merely negative voices that are kept from being curses when you accept emptying out and learn to play the notes shattering the darkness.

Golf teaches that a God who is personal with you can even use golf to show that Jesus came to convince you that his power is alive and Satan's power with abuse inside it is ending. But we have to keep believing to understand this powerful lesson. We must truly believe and we must empty out the negative voices so they won't become curses.

Believing

When I coached baseball at Bishop O'Connell High School in Arlington, Virginia, I had a player named Sean Gallagher. Sean later attended Wake Forest University on a baseball scholarship. One day I asked Sean how he was able to hit all those home runs when he was only 5'8" and 150 pounds. I asked him how he was able to release that bat so smoothly. You know what he said? Sean told me, "I don't know Mr. Steib, but I know I will do it again"—a great answer about believing. Fifteen years later at the O'Connell alumni tournament, I saw Sean again and told him that story. You know what? Sean won the long drive contest in the tournament. He still believed.

We must restore belief again to our young people and search for ways like golf to show people that believing can break the power of evil trying to get inside us. We must, like Sean, learn to believe that the good we have accomplished in the past will repeat itself again and again in the future. But in a larger, faster, freer world, believing is the only way we can end abuse. Belief is the light that comes from the end of the tunnel. It's what tells you the flow will always be about the ball rolling in the fairway, even when it doesn't. Like Sean, we can say, "Why not me?" If it happened once before, it can happen again and again. But we must sense we are believing. When we learn to believe, we will get that tempo of trust we need in our lives. Golf has taught me that the tempo in our swings can make you believe that there can be God's tempo in our lives, once we learn to let go and let God. Once we learn to accept belief as a pathway in our lives and reject nonbelieving, we will begin to experience the tempo of the good coming around the bend.

Learning from Golf, or What Golf Can Teach

Golf can teach you that in the twenty-first century, humankind no longer has to feel deserted. The world we experience today is no longer defined by maps of religion and race. Life today is a journey into the unknown. No round of golf is a true story before it is real. Unless you experience the light breaking into the power of evil on the course, you will never comprehend being on a journey, not on the golf course and not in life itself. Moreover, you will never know you are a released person. You don't play the game of golf to stay out of traps. You play the game of golf to exercise the confidence you have in your ability to make good shots and avoid bad ones.

You will never put the ball in the hole if it is necessary to have abuse inside you to maintain peace, or if you have to keep practicing your poor shots before you can make good ones. If the power of war, if the power of your bad shots has not already been broken, you won't be making your journey through a glass lightly. You will never get out of the glass darkly. Beginning with the Lord in the New Testament, all of us meet special people in our lives. Humanity won't save us. God making humanity and golf special in our lives can save us. Jesus is our personal savior and uses everything.

Recently, at the school where I teach, Bishop Denis J. O'Connell High School, we put on the play *West Side Story*. My good friend Bob Guerin played the character Doc. Doc ran a drug store that was a hangout for the various gangs in the neighborhood. Doc would resolve arguments and break up gang fights, but Doc was always saddened by what he saw. Once he said after a fight scene, "Stop it, stop it. What have you been doing now? What does it take to get through to you? When do you stop? You make this world lousy." Now, *West Side Story* is set in the 1950s. Imagine the desertion people felt in the1950s. Was life a journey then? How could it be a journey when people were always deserted? How long could they stay in a deserted state of mind? Reality was that the world was "lousy." Abuse was in everyone's nature. If you played golf, feeling deserted had to be why you practiced long hours at your swing. There wasn't the sense that something was always out there to be noticed, adding life to freedom. If that were true, the feeling of being deserted could have been the beginning of wisdom. Why? Because instead of *desertion,* the new word could be *flow.* God, in other words, can use desertion to give you patience until you begin to be in the flow. Then, losing your swing doesn't have to be an empty feeling.

Players of Note

Does flow come from a work ethic? I believe true release is flow without abuse having any part in it. Flow is trusting that no bogey has a hold on you. Every shot you practice has no divots inside it. Sure, you miss shots, but in golf you must learn the flow of the shot while you empty out the missed shots. Probably the greatest work ethic of any golfer in history was that of Ben Hogan. It's been said that Ben learned the game in the dirt. If bad shots were accidents, it was because Ben made hitting five hundred balls a day the reason for his success. When Ben Hogan was in a trap, he didn't walk with faith. He got the ball out of the trap because of the five hundred practice balls he hit each day. He was, of course, one of golf's greatest players, but how different was Hogan from Arnold Palmer, Jack Nicklaus, Tom Watson, Lee Trevino, Gary Player, or Tiger Woods? These players hit the decades between the '60s and the '90s like light breaking into a storm. They likely didn't view practice as a way to get out of divots. They understood practice to be a method of breaking the power the divots had over them. Arnie never worried about the consequences. He was the first to take the shortest route between two points.

Jack Nicklaus, unlike Arnie, played the game very cerebrally. But like Arnie, he too played without thorns in his flesh. He missed shots, but, for Jack, missed shots were accidents. His intelligence had already broken the power of the missed shot. Jack believed in the power of release to break his wayward shots on the course. Jack's good swings were like music to his ears, playing out inside his head.

One of the first psychological players was Tom Watson. Who can forget his great shot on the seventeenth hole in the 1982 U.S. Open? Tom dreamed that shot into the hole. Lee Trevino was another psychological player. He often won tournaments with putters he found in pawnshops or someone's attic. Lee could always see the future coming to him. He never covered anything up in his game. The merry Mexican believed.

Gary Player would never shop in an attic. He'd rather be the thorn in your flesh with his training and rigorous work ethic. He was a definite throwback to Ben Hogan. Both Ben and Gary, however, never gave up. They always persevered. It's just that for them the light was always at the end of the tunnel. It didn't keep coming, breaking the hold the power of the tunnel has.

Finally, we reach the megastar of the now: Tiger Woods. Tiger plays the game without fear, as if there is no fear inside his being. Yes, he gets angry at times. But, it's always a power being broken. He never lets his bad shot put him on a map. His new nature without abuse, which he always trusts in tight situations, keeps him in a flow. Notice that whenever the pressure is on Tiger, he acquires that focus. He does not mess with his swing or engage in idle talk. Tiger seems certain that his next shot is without thorns. There is only release from the end of the tunnel, lighting his path time after time. Tiger's character is truly defined by his thornless greatness, not by the abuse inside him that he is overcoming. He knows any power that thorns might have has already been broken.

For centuries, people played games to escape the world. They had to overcome the world inside them to hit the shots. But suppose you can play like Tiger, not the world. What would that mean? It would mean you played the game of golf in the *word*. It would mean you played the game of golf without the letter *l* in the word *world*. The word with golf inside it is real. The world golf is teaching is unreal unless you take out the letter *l*. Tiger plays the game in the "word." Mike Wynn says Tiger Woods surpasses everyone with his mind-set. This was certainly evident when Tiger won his fourth major championship.

So what else does Mike say is so special about Tiger Woods? He says it's Tiger's ability to stay tall through the ball to the finish—taller than anyone, Mike says, who has ever played the game. Why is height so important? Well, Mike says, the club stops at impact if you go after the ball with your legs. In doing so, you will also start picking the clubhead up at address, and that will keep you from being away from the ball in the swing.

Flow vs. Timing

The meaning of being away, the key to flow, is learning to swing away in your feet. If you lose your height, you will lack the extension you need so that the club can release on its own and so that the finish to the swing can happen. This has always been a serious flaw for me in my swing. For years, I played baseball, and I was a contact hitter. The way that I swung, the bat stopped moving on impact with the ball. The same problem has happened to me in my golf swing. The motion of my body stops at impact and doesn't keep moving to the finish of the swing. In effect, I'm a punch hitter of the golf ball, and I have trouble with my follow-through. I've found I can't remember to finish from the top, or beginning, of my swing, because, if I do, the finish doesn't happen. I can't really think at all because, when I play this game, my eyes have to always be opening,or I start blinking. For finish to happen, release has to free the club. I can't release the club if the motion of my body stops at impact. My problem is getting the negative thoughts out of my mind before I finish my swing. Why can't I move my address position through to the finish? Mike says it was because I needed balance in my swing. The problem is that no matter how hard Mike taught me, a "cross" inside me needed to be broken before his lesson could have any effect.

Then, one day on the driving range, release came in the form of my friend, Terry Cronin. He said I swung the club with great timing but no flow. "I thought timing was flow," I told Terry. He said that was wrong and that timing and flow are intertwined yet very different in expression. By emphasizing timing, I was putting pressure on the way I held the club. What would happen is that I would end up grabbing the club and sucking it inside on my backswing. When I did that with my hands, Mike told me, it caused my left shoulder to tilt and my left knee to go down at the start of my backswing—a reverse weight shift, which is a big no-no in golf. I began to understand why I went down with my body at impact, why I had to always stop at address before finishing, and why my club couldn't release. I simply had no flow. For years, I thought timing was flow. Now, I had to start all over again and learn flow in my swing. Imagine, for fifty-six years, I never swung the golf club—never lived my life. I was beginning to feel deserted. But now, it was a different deserted feeling. Release wasn't at the end of the tunnel. Release was the light from the end of the tunnel. Release was getting me into the flow.

If I wanted to cover up my flow with timing, I could, but my consequence would be a total lack of freedom, which can only come from the flow. But what is flow? Is it motion? Mike says flow is softness from the beginning to the finish of the swing. You must have soft arms hanging down from you shoulders, maintaining your height all the way to the finish. As I said earlier, Mike teaches you all the mechanics you are using that make you tense. If you truly are soft, the timing of the swing happens. You don't have to make it happen. The problem is that most people go to pros to add more mechanics, which immediately takes them out of their flow, which in turn throws off their timing. For fourteen years, I kept adopting Mike's mechanics to enhance my poor mechanics. I was covering up my lack of tempo with more mechanical thoughts. As a result, I could not get released, because I lacked the softness to release me. I needed more open heart surgery on my being so that "faith" in my swing could set me free.

Trust

You see, Mike Wynn teaches that the game is a total commitment to trust. There are no swing planes, no swing thoughts, and no secrets—only awareness of those mechanical thoughts that keep you from not swinging in a flow. A good pro can identify those thoughts, but you can't keep substituting the pro's thoughts for your own. Mike told me the tension in my arms comes when my arms aren't relaxed at address, when they don't maintain height or don't hang straight down, the clubhead will not go back properly in the swing. Soft arms and feet create flow and a winding motion. The timing has already happened in the softness. Once you begin to trust the softness as the faith being released inside you, you will begin to sense the window for release that is always there within you. Your choice becomes whether you want to believe or end up living a cursed existence.

Living a Cursed Life

There are essentially two ways you can live a cursed life. You can believe excellence is not already here releasing us and not be able to release because you cursed yourself, or you can leave it all up to yourself in a "survival of the fittest" universe which has abuse inside it. Whether you live in a glass darkly or are burdening yourself, all of your existence is your choice. You can see life as a journey or you can end up living a cursed life on a map.

Until I played golf, I had faced life by cursing the day I was born, never even knowing I was doing that to myself. Somewhere along the way, you can't go on in a cursed existence on earth. You need a life without the curse inside it. You need to know release is coming to you. Golf was part of the release coming to me. But I still had yet to commit myself to the good already here. I still had to end the curse inside myself before I could be released.

What I've learned is that humility originates in the awesomeness of God's love, releasing us when we accept emptying out as part of our nature. Like Tiger Woods, we no longer have to live cursed lives to be humble. That is false humility. What we need to do is trust that a greater power always turns our red lights into green ones. Every shot we take on the course has been put there for us to make it so that we can know that we are loved and can be totally committed to love.

In a 2001 *Parade* magazine article entitled, "Now I Understand What's Sacred," Sylvester Stallone says that early in his life he climbed every mountain because his understanding of life was that to be successful you have to put your mind and body through every obstacle in your path. But what he found out was that his life was getting narrower and narrower and that he didn't feel good about himself. He had a cursed existence while attaining his success. Stallone says he enjoys life again because he now understands what is sacred. He realizes how much mountain is mountain enough. He says that he now has a sense of invincibility, that when he walks into a room and his children are present, he feels a sense of timelessness with them. In other words, his children always turn red lights into green lights. He is humbled by their presence. He is no longer cursed because, in his children, he sees people without a curse. Stallone has learned, as I have in golf, that the mind and the heart need to be transcended by a reality without a curse inside it.

Mike Wynn, on the golf course, represents a person like that for me because he never had the curses inside his swing that I had inside mine. Could that be true in life? Jesus came to earth to break the hold that the power of evil has over people. Since Jesus's time, many other people have also come to release the earth from its curse.

Release from a Cursed Life

Golf has taught me that if a pro can feel release, it's possible that God releases us all the time from our cursed world. All we have to do is open our hearts to the Gospel and see his power ending the curses inside people the way Mike Wynn ended the curses inside my golf swing. The problem for so many people, however, is that they can't believe without believing they are cursed on earth. The have to commit themselves, like Tiger Woods, to believing the glory without curses is here right now and go for it. When Tiger Woods gets ahead, he never backs up. Nothing can ever back him up. He makes mistakes, but he never lets his errors define him. He is available to others, but he has no time for people who don't want to pursue excellence without the curse. If you have any doubts or if you believe only in yourself, then you will be no match for Tiger Woods. His freedom is his birthright and has overcome his dark side. Tiger never allows his dark side to put him on a map. The power of the dark side has been broken forever by people who don't have curses inside them, going back to the death of Jesus on the cross.

Finding a Driver

I have recently experienced great problems in finding a driver. Every driver has a little different feel. Frankly, drivers are like cups of coffee. No two of them taste identical. So for years I struggled to find one. One man I kept believing would have the driver I wanted was a man named Jim Smiley. He owned an exotic golf shop in Manassas, Virginia. I won't tell you how much money I paid that man, but I really believed I would find a driver in his shop. Then, one day, I had him put a new KZG head on a driver I saw in his used club barrel. Just as I was going out the door, I saw an interesting driver mixed up with other drivers in the barrel. I asked Smiley about this driver, and he said it was a new SP700 head KZG was making. I immediately told him that I wanted to buy this one. Smiley made another one. I had my new club, and out I went to play. This would be the real McCoy!

There is a game we play on individual holes called "Throwing Down the GW," in which a dollar bill becomes the wager for a long drive challenge. A friend of mine, Floyd Foley, is a competitor who always likes the challenge of a GW. Well, my time was now, so I threw down my GW on the fifteenth hole and let my new KZG driver set me free. Would you believe I outdrove Mr. Foley for the first time in months? I really ripped it; I have to be honest. Floyd "let me have it" on the next two holes, but I won the long drive once, and I know I could do it again. And that's release, knowing it can happen again. I bought that driver from Smiley because I liked the way he believed in release. Smiley knew the feeling of flow in his clubs. I knew the right club was inside his shop. I only had to believe. I believed his shop wasn't cursed. Therefore, I knew the driver of my dreams would be in his shop. For me, his shop was part of the sacred universe. I learned that the heart is the key to both believing and not living a cursed life. Golf began to teach me that the flow is in the heart that believes, but I needed one last lesson.

Club Face

Later in our friendship, Mike found work at South Wales Golf Club in Virginia, and I caught up with him there. I asked Mike about keeping the clubface toward the target. He immediately asked me why I would want to think about the clubface; in other words, why would I always want to know where it was going. He said, "There you go again. You aren't trusting that the clubface already knows where it is going to go. You have to get out of the way and let it go there." He said, "Finish the swing. Don't worry about the target." He said worrying about the target and the clubface would make me ball- and target-bound. In so doing, I would lose my softness and get in the way of where the clubface wants to go on its own. I asked Mike why I was afraid the ball wouldn't go to the target. Why was I afraid? Because I wasn't a released person? Why wasn't I released? I mean, it had been fifteen years, and I still didn't know the meaning of release in my being. I still was ball- and target-bound.

Think of how in my larger, faster, freer universe people are becoming ball- and target-bound. We have seen how communism tried to make the human being bigger that God. We have seen how talented people become larger than their talent. We have seen religious leaders in the twentieth century who believe God is bigger than they are, but who still lack an appreciation for life having meaning before you die in the same way it will be meaningful after you die. Many people still do not understand how God shares his being with everyone who doesn't make himself larger than God, or who doesn't make himself larger than his or her talent. God is being, and he used golf to reveal his being to me so that I would learn to give freedom a chance.

How Much Abuse Is Enough?

Freedom in the twenty-first century is supernatural, and golf teaches me that the scenarios I have made for myself on the golf course can be broken if I give being a chance. But what is being? Being is learning to accept emptying yourself out as necessary for the light to come from the end of the tunnel. Hence, if you give emptying out a chance you are giving a God who is free a chance. "With God, all things are possible," the saying goes. For the first time, God could share his being with me on the golf course, in church, in my work and with my friends. Life in the future doesn't have to be about putting people in scenarios, on maps where death keeps repeating itself. Jesus has ended the abuse in our nature. We are free when we give him a chance and learn the emptying out that leads to grace, not the discipline that keeps correcting mistakes on a map and leaves us full of abuse.

I began to see how, when you give emptying out a chance on the golf course, you won't keep repeating your mistakes, your poor shots. Golf, when I didn't make myself bigger than the game and when I knew God shared his being with me (i.e., didn't treat me as though I were in a scenario). Golf, when you get it right, has no scenarios. The key to golf is to get in the flow. The key to life is to recognize the flow and go with it as it takes your clubface to the target. The problem is, I still wasn't flowing in my swing. I was still ball- and target-bound. I was still fighting something. And who or what was I fighting? I was fighting my understanding that the game is bigger than me. I wasn't listening to Mike. I still hadn't grasped his message completely. I was learning that I needed to listen to the truth that sets us free. We have to listen to our mentors, to the roots, as they are passed on to us to deliver to others.

Wholeness in the Big Picture

No one is bigger than God, but God creates us in his image, and we aren't made to be junk. We are created to be free in the spiritual choices God gives us to complete the full swing and be whole. When Adam and Eve committed their original sin, Satan, who is fighting something, got inside of them and is still in us today. But the good news is that golf has taught me that the power of evil is conquered when you get the attitude of giving the God who shares his being with us a chance. God is pure love, with no hate at all for any creatures. He wants to win our hearts, not clone us with his mind. His son's resurrection has ended the power that fights inside us and has replaced this power of darkness with a new empowerment of the glass lightly.

With this new empowerment, the coward's heart can never get to our wholeness and never lets wholeness be broken by fear. So why was I ball- and target-bound? Why did I let the ball and target become the scenario that kept me out of the flow? Because I was out of the flow, my scenario kept causing me to dive into the ball and suck the club into my body. When I pulled the butt end of the club into my body, my weight always went onto my back foot.

I asked Mike about the problem, and he said that in order to avoid pulling the club inside on my back swing, I was taking the club too far outside. What he wanted me to do is work the club gradually inside to the top of the backswing. That seemed to work well, but then I told Mike that perhaps I didn't pull the club into my body. Maybe I was diving into the clubhead. As that point, Mike could see that, after all these years, I still was fighting the big picture. I was fighting the roots going back to the works of the Father. But was it Mike I was fighting, or something inside me that made me think I was bigger than God? I was beginning to recognize the original sin in me. I began to see how ball- and target-bound I had become. I simply had no being from God in my soul and was living in a scenario.

Well, Mike said that never in fifteen years had I really trusted the motion he was giving me without any mistakes inside it. Mike told me to only turn right and left with all the parts working together and drive the ball. He told me not to worry about pulling the club into my body on the downswing. He never showed me that motion so why should I think I was doing it? He said to trust the right and left motion with your feet and don't think about performing the correct motion, and you won't pull the club inside. Don't try to make the positive correct the negative. I was beginning to see now that my whole life was doing good deeds so that I wouldn't do bad ones. I had never believed in a flow of the Holy Spirit in my life that could get me from the right side to the left side without worrying about my mistakes. A true flow of the water always running when I accepted emptying out is not a curse.

A New Outlook on Life

Golf taught me a new outlook on life. God showers his mercy and freedom on us at all times, and we should learn to live in the flow he gives us, through his son, the way we learn to go right and left in the swing—total freedom. Sure, we will still make mistakes, but once we are in the flow, the big picture will erase them altogether. We no longer have to correct them to get into the big picture. Our relationship to the Lord going back to the works of the Father will save us. We just have to accept the emptying out as not being a curse, but a release.

Mike said to simply turn, finish, and maintain your height. Move everything backward and forward. This motion isn't the result of trial and error. For Mike, that motion he shows you is the correct one. His is not basing his motion on correcting your mistakes. His motion is always in the glass lightly, where all of your mistakes are erased without a new motion that does not have mistakes.

I've learned in golf that you never get out of the scenario if you don't know what it means to live in the flow. You haven't learned that a flow from the light at the end of the tunnel has broken all of your scenarios.

We live in a world today in which people need to believe in the intent inside the heart that is connected to the works of the Father. This is no longer a Shakespearean world where people don't have to believe. The Bard's world was glass darkly. It was tragic. The glass lightly couldn't shatter the darkness due to dualism in nature. To me, Shakespeare didn't communicate the light at the end of the tunnel as on the other side now. Golf—not Shakespeare—does that for me. This is a Shakespearean world in which all life will be a tragedy if we continue to live in scenarios and don't see the light from the end of the tunnel breaking them. All of my life I have been taught that I have been going to a light at the end of the tunnel. On the way to the light, I had to worry always about not getting there. Now golf was teaching me that the light from the end of the tunnel is there the more you trust and give emptying out and the notes from being a chance. Until you give being a chance in a new motion where you don't have to worry about your mistakes, release will never happen, because you will always be in your own way.

For the first time, I was beginning to understand how original sin keeps you in the glass darkly. It never lets you forget your mistakes because you always have to correct them to make progress. The good news is that, in Christ, a new motion without mistakes has been given to you so you can be a released person. When Mike taught me that turn-finish motion, I forgot about how I was correcting my mistakes. I just turned and finished my swing and believed more each time in the new motion, until the light from the end of the tunnel was my swing.

I was finally beginning to understand that God intends all people to be free and without memory of their mistakes. We still make mistakes, but with faith, we know our mistakes have no power over us. We trust more, not less. If you complete your swing remembering your mistakes, you will always *be going* to the light at the end of the tunnel. You would never get there. That is why God is larger than we are. That is why we make God's creation too small. We are not meant to be nothing. God continually shares himself with us every moment of our existence. God is free, and he wants us to be free. We will be free if we never allow ourselves to be larger than God, yet believe he created us to reflect his being. He wants us to reflect his glory. He wants us to be empowered by this vision in a larger, faster, freer world instead of ruling people with authority, which is always worried about mistakes. He wants authority to learn a motion that only has the freedom of the works of the Father inside it. We would learn together how the Holy Spirit makes being supernatural on earth and how more and more people will give God a chance because they know he is free.

For those who want to keep living in scenarios, the flow will never set them free. Instead of controlling people's lives inside scenarios, authority figures, such as parents and teachers, need to learn to lead by helping people stay in the flow the way Mike helped me in the flow of my swing.

I could now see why Mike said the swing is all about trust. God intends for us to trust his universe as friendly. He gives us everyday people we must learn to trust. If you can't trust, you are still trying to correct your mistakes with good swings. You are still inside the box and have not learned how to live in the glass lightly. Imagine a world outside the box, trusting the motion of the spirit breaking the scenarios that are keeping us in the dark until we know we are free. For centuries people were afraid to choose in the spirit.

Golf has taught me that there is fluid motion. God is free, and he projects his freedom onto us at every moment. His being is a flow with no darkness inside it. As a matter of fact, after I listened to Mike about believing in the flow, I knew how the clubhead could already have started. It was in the flow from the moment

I gripped the club. The flow is everything going backward and forward through the ball.

Once we realize that his sea is so great and that our boat is so small, we only have to learn to trust the motion he gives us. We only have to learn the flow without any mistakes. We will still make bad swings, but golf taught me that there can always be a new motion that can help you put your mistakes behind you. You no longer have to keep a scenario intact. The box will keep you out of the flow.

Golf teaches you that there are no scenarios with mistakes inside them. There are only choices that are supernatural and connected by epiphanies. Man is free. He only has to want to be free and to let the flow release him.

You see, for Mike, trust is the key factor. You have to believe in the big picture and know where the clubface is going. Otherwise, you end up playing golf with a small mind. You won't have the softness to let the clubface go where it wants to go. You will have a cursed swing on the golf course because the big picture won't be there to win your heart with notes from being when you empty out.

The idea of release in golf is to keep your softness so that the big picture will always keep the mechanics from giving you a small mind. Softness is trust! Release, believing you are loved by an authority shatters your darkness so you can be released on the other side now. Remember, golf is not so much about discipline as it is about keeping your attention focused when you empty out. The heart in golf is your belief in the big picture keeping you from having a small mind, keeping you from being cloned.

It was interesting at the 2002 Masters to see how Vijay Singh worried so much about the mud on the ball. When they asked Tiger, the mud on the ball didn't let his mind get small. He mentioned that the mud on the ball spins the ball in a certain direction and will require adjusting your swing. Tiger never lets his problems make the mind small. He always sees the big picture without the curse inside it. When the other players seemed to curse their games on Sunday, Tiger kept moving farther ahead. He never backed up to the field. The more he committed himself to shots without curses, the more his competitors set him free while they kept drowning in their own abuse.

What golf should teach us is that there is a big picture without a curse inside it. We are all called to stay out of irreconcilable situations without compromising our true selves. Tiger will always be there for people. If people want to keep playing cursed games of golf, however, Tiger will pass them by on his journey into the love of God now, not later.

Think of the world prior to World War I. No one thought in the big picture. Men lived cursed lives. There was no larger picture keeping minds from getting small. People lived and acted in a cursed world as a rule, not the exception, which kept the negative always coming around. There was no trust that the cursed world as a rule had already been broken by the blood of Jesus so that people could believe in a big picture without a curse.

It took Woodrow Wilson's Fourteen Points to finally establish a big picture, ending the glass darkly as a rule so mankind could have hope. Wilson's Fourteen Points were glass lightly. God used them to gather us into his kingdom on the other side now. They were doors opening to larger doors. Without the Fourteen Points, would Tiger and Vijay been able to be gathered in by God? For the first time, people answered not to their leaders, but to the truth. It was then up to leaders to reflect the truth that followed them. It was the truth that kept evil from having power over us. The world, and America in specific, was compassionate for the first time in history.

Golf has taught me the meaning of the big picture. Now, I can trust my mind not to get small because I know from golf that a big picture exists. You just have to believe. And believing, I've learned, is what keeps your game from being cursed. Golf teaches us how to move on while resting. Tiger Woods never gives into a cursed worldview. As a rule, he doesn't have time to be around people who want to accept cursed lives. He knows that a big picture does exist without a curse inside it, so that man won't be defined by a small mind. Tiger commits himself to the excellence already here for him from the works of the Father.

The question in golf is why they play the game with small minds. Why? Because they aren't soft enough. Before the clubhead can get into position, you have to know what it is to be soft when you address the ball. The big picture is the larger (science), faster (speed and industry), and freer (politics) universe unfolding God inside us and around us. Golf is one aspect of this evolving authority that gives us freedom and our life meaning. You have to know that the big picture, trusting in your golf swing, is what will always keep your game from giving you a small mind. Well, what is the big picture you trust in the golf swing that makes you soft?

For Mike Wynn, the big picture is knowing that the clubface will release without any hands on the club. How, you might ask, can that happen. No hands on club? You have to be kidding. Well, Mike asked me how I had been taught to make a backswing. I said with my shoulders and arms taking the club away in my backswing. Why? Mike asked. I said, "Because you told me to trigger my swing with my shoulders." "No," Mike said, "I told you to trigger the swing with everything being soft." "How," I asked, "can everything be soft?" Now for the first time, I began to see how Mike could remain soft throughout his swing. He had no backswing to make him hard. He could never be rigid because there were no arms, shoulders, or hands starting the swing which made him rigid. Mike swung the club freely because there was nothing to inhibit his freedom. You might ask, "How, then, did Mike start the swing? Didn't he need his shoulders, hips, hands, and arms to start the swing?" No, not at all. All Mike needed to believe was that freedom making him soft is what starts the swing. The swing is generated by freedom, and freedom makes you soft. Hence, your desire to be free is what makes you soft, starts your swing, and is what puts the club in position.

I asked Mike where the desire to be free originates, and he said it was in the heart. "Do you mean," I asked Mike, "that the heart starts the swing?" He told me that it absolutely does; the heart is what has to believe that life is a flow, not a scenario. The heart has to trust that the motion back and forth is all you have to do. It's the heart which has to trust that the softness in your arms is what puts the club into the flow. In other words, golf has to win your heart before you can be soft. Mike said that the only awareness he has in the golf swing is in where the ball is going. He has no awareness of the position of the clubface. He doesn't even want to let his feet stick to the ground. He wants everything to be soft at address. "Well," I said to Mike, "I still don't know what triggers me in my freedom to start the swing." Mike then told me that I still don't understand release if I ask that question. "Why?" I asked. "Because," he said, "if you released the club just once, you would want to start the club again so you could experience that freedom one more time."

The Flow

Golf teaches us the power of freedom in our world. It's the engine God gave us,through his son, that starts everything. Release is freedom. Release is believing Freedom is what keeps creation and your golf swing in motion. You are released when you know that being soft is what makes release happen and you want to experience release again and again. Right now in my game, I am just getting to where my desire to be free is the communication with the Father, which is waking up my heart so I can start my swing. Imagine a scenario where no mistakes need to be corrected, where there is only fluid motion with no thinking about the negative inside it, only a born-again motion. At last I was free in my softness to start my swing. Mike took away the last thing I needed to know, which had been making me tense: He took away my mistake-driven mind-set. There aren't any mistakes.

Now, all I have to do when I start my swing is finish what I've started. Why finish? Because finishing your swing while remaining soft is all you can do. In fact, I might even say there is no swing. There is only flow at address. The everything is the light at the end of the tunnel. In finally getting there, so that we know the target is always larger, even when we fail, we know there are no mistakes.

The purpose of the swing is to finish the flow. The golf swing is all about flowing or finishing the everything, which is always in the present moment and is always there. Once I began to finish the takeaway, I stopped releasing the club at the bottom of the swing. I simply finished the everything by turning and returning. I could feel the sensation of the clubhead winding the body gradually inside to the top of the backswing, until the flow was finished and the hands finally released. I was seeing release take me across the lake and I know the emptying out could be the water always running to win my heart.

God had used golf to show me the glory he showed the apostles when he and his son took the disciples across the lake. Remember that story? Jesus had already said he wanted to go across the lake, and still, when the storm came up, his disciples didn't believe him. But notice what Jesus did next. He told his disciples to be still. Be at rest. In other words, be soft. He didn't tell the storm or waves or wind to be still. These forces of nature were still only after the apostles became soft. It's

112

the same way with the golf swing. You have to be at peace before the clubhead can go where it wants to go and the curse in your swing can finally end. You have to trust absolutely in the softness and freedom of the address position before you can finish the flow. Once you finish the flow, the clubface has taken you across the lake.

Would you want to go across the lake again? I would. Already having finished your flow is knowing the release is not about you. It's about the love of the Father for you. It's about knowing you are not alone in a larger, faster, freer universe. It's Isaiah 30:15: "Be at peace. Be still and you will be saved." Why? Because release is always coming to free you. And once you know there is release, you want to be part of that release so others will notice and be set free; so others won't live with small minds. You want others to notice that a big picture releases them in the way it releases you.

This is exactly what I experienced in my lessons with Mike Wynn. He had release for me in the golf swing. For the first time, Mike showed me how to notice the subtleties in a golf swing and on a golf course. When you're on a map, you are in a cursed world. You are not soft enough to notice these subtleties. It's just life not being soft enough in your setup. When you're not soft enough at address, the club simply won't take you where it wants to take you.

Learning to swing the club with no hands, no backswing, and no downswing is the big picture you have to trust. Everything makes the backswing and downswing one piece. Without the big picture in your swing, you won't get the clubhead into position. It takes heart to believe in the big picture. It takes heart to trust that your swing will get you across the lake when you can't feel it. You need to notice anything that creeps into your swing that keeps you from trusting, keeping you from being soft. There are no new mechanics. There is only your setup, and finishing the flow.

Great Teacher of the Flow

I had just gotten out of the Army and was applying to graduate school when my applications were returned with the results. Only one person wrote me a handwritten letter and invited me up to the University of Oregon to study for a master's degree in interdisciplinary studies. The other four applications returned with form letters from the institutions where I was rejected. Only Professor Lloyd Sorenson, who was like Mike Wynn, wrote me a handwritten letter of acceptance. This man was responsible for giving me a thirty-year teaching career at Bishop O'Connell High School. He was a glass lightly in my life, shattering my personal darkness, but I was still learning that the target was already larger.

Why had it taken me so long to notice a letter from being? It came out of nowhere and saved my life. Release happens because the target is already larger; that's why we say release to each other. I think it's because I hadn't yet learned how to think, to ask questions. I still lived on a map with my small mind. When I faced adversity, I let the map make my mind smaller. I hadn't yet learned how to believe in my heart that the big picture is always there, when I empty out my false self. It took golf to awaken my heart to the big picture, never letting me put myself in a box because of my negative thoughts, but always emptying out until I could trust that being would show up.

As we discussed earlier, one person who always seemed to understand the big picture was Arnold Palmer. Once I was at the Congressional Country Club in Potomac, Maryland, watching Arnie play in the Senior Open. When Arnie got to the first tee, there were people lined up six deep all the way to the green on both sides of the fairway. When Arnie emerged from the crowd around the tee, he was dressed resplendently again in a gold shirt and grey slacks. He truly looked like the king in all his glory when he came through the ropes, protected on all sides by policemen.

When Arnie addressed the ball, it seemed as though all time slowed down as the crowd's noise came to a total silence. Even more remarkable was how the sun came out from behind the clouds at the precise moment of impact, to paint a glorious picture. And you know what? I noticed the phenomenon. All eyes on the course that day were opened to majesty because they saw an example of profound release. God knew his people were there, so he used Arnie's faith to proclaim God's glory and make it a special day for all of us. Arnie walked out of the glory to help each one of us believe that we can all rise through our trials and tribulations. We just have to believe in the big picture keeping our minds from getting small.

Some people who play golf never get lessons or notice ways in which they could improve. At some point, the abuse of not knowing makes you wonder how much abuse is abuse enough. How long can I keep the big picture out and live in a cursed world before I give up the game? Well, the good news is that golf will always have its Mike Wynns and Arnold Palmers. You and I only have to believe, and believing is the meaning of release.

Ending

I'd like to end this book by saying that golf has taught me that life is never over until it's over. We, the people of the world, are all on a journey much like the eighteen-hole golf course. Some people on the journey notice the big picture releasing them, by keeping their lives from going into a bottomless pit caused by original sin. Those people are the believers, the ones who notice the subtleties being given to them to help them believe the journey is heaven over them. These are the Tiger Woods or Arnold Palmers, who never let the negative voice make their lives a bottomless pit. Others in the world only see the journey as a cursed life. They never realize a larger picture always present, not throwing them into a bottomless pit. You often see these latter players throwing the club behind them from the start. They possess no soft, true motion. Actually, the journey on the golf course will only be heaven over you when you decide the bigger picture is always present, and learn to receive it day by day as it is given you. The journey is discovering that the game of golf is not out to throw you into a bottomless pit.

The goal of this book has been to show you that release is possible before you die because life is always a journey helping you believe God loves you. When you understand this, then you begin to notice a true story he is giving you each moment of your life. Until you can believe your journey on the golf course is heaven over you, you will never be released when you play golf. Why? Because the journey is only for those who believe that each person's heart is inside a being who surpasses all understanding. Without a heart that empties out in a larger, faster, freer world, we will be left without ourselves. Golf has taught me that an accursed self can't live in this life. There will still be traps on your journey, but the difference is that you will know that the big picture never lets your traps throw you into a bottomless pit. The traps are part of the emptying out you need to do to see the notes that being wants you to have in your heart.

For me, golf is a glimpse of heaven that keeps me out of the bottomless pit of original sin when I experience release. Golf is part of heaven somewhere else and here at the same time. The only reason we can't always see heaven with golf inside it releasing us now is because of original sin, or the negative voice inside all of us. The trick is to translate the negative voice into a journey, until you realize the big picture, with release inside it, is already here, never letting the negative voice make you small. Like Tiger Woods, you must learn to receive what is put there before you, with a total commitment to God's love breaking into your life. Any doubt is blinking. We must learn to play the game of life where it lies with our eyes always open to the light because we have a heart that has learned to accept emptying out the dark side.

When my father passed away in 1993, I experienced death for the first time. My dad, Bart Sr., was filled with cancer, very weak, and without much weight in his body. When my mother and I returned home on the evening of his death, we found a picture of my dad in an Evergreen Golf jacket. We never knew that my dad had taken that picture, but it was there, mixed in with all his other pictures in his bedroom closet. When we used this picture at the wake, many people remarked how good my dad looked in the picture. He was around sixty at the time it was taken. When I looked at that picture, I knew my dad was released. I knew that he was telling my mom and me that he was released from all the disease that had racked his body. My dad's picture was the kingdom somewhere else and here simultaneously, keeping me from going into the bottomless pit. In that moment, I know all the lights were green.

Is it true for Tiger Woods that all his lights are green? Perhaps our journey will only end when we know without a doubt, with our eyes fully opened, that the power that turns the red light on has been turned off. The trick is to believe that the big picture is a green light that has turned off all the power of the red lights in our life. When that happens, eternity won't be somewhere else. It will be the light breaking into our lives, turning off all power of the red light until we know we have been released. If it weren't for golf, I would never have known God's tempo, revealing to me his image and likeness in my being. I would never have known that released golfers can be released people, people like Marianne Williamson, who writes these words in her book *A Return to Love*:

> Our deepest fear is that we are powerful beyond our measure. It is our light, not our darkness, that most frightens us. We ask ourselves, who am I to be brilliant, gorgeous, talented, fabulous? Actually, who are you not to be? You are a child of God. Your playing small does not serve the world. There is nothing enlightened about shrinking so that other people won't feel insecure around you…. We were born to make manifest the glory of God that is within us.

EPILOGUE

OK, you've read the book. Did you figure out the meaning of the dream regarding Alvin Dark? Did you perceive the dream coming to you as you read through the subtopics? Did you begin to recognize any epiphanies in your own thinking as the meaning of the dream was being revealed to you?

Well, here it is. ALVIN DARK is a kind of acronym for "All LoVe is IN DARKness." Why? To learn the golf swing, you have to see the game as part of a journey coming to you. Golf is not about egos or winning games. It's also not about belief making golf a thorn in the flesh where the game is played in a glass darkly. No, you should have seen that golf is about trusting the journey that is always revealing itself to you in all aspects of your life. Obviously everyone makes mistakes, but on the golf course, don't allow your mistakes to become curses. Learn to accept your mistakes until the journey that has already corrected them reveals their solution to you. In other words, learn to empty out in darkness until the beautiful mind of God makes you whole on your journey.

Recently, my friends, Tom and Charlie, and I played golf with Mike Wynn at the Stonewall Golf Club in Gainesville, Virginia. Tom was playing his best round ever until he came to the eighteenth hole—a par five with water and a sand trap on the right side. Well, Tom unexpectedly struck his ball off to the right and into the water. It was his first really errant shot of the round. Incidentally, it didn't keep Tom from shooting 73 that day, but Charlie, Mike, and I wondered how he put the shot into the water after he had played so well over seventeen holes.

We asked Mike, and he said, "Tom didn't have a target in mind when he made his swing."

I asked Mike a familiar question: "How can you release the club if you have to guide your swing to the target?"

Mike answered me with a question. He asked, "At what target do you think I'm aiming?"

I replied that it might be a spot in the fairway, maybe a house or a tree or a smoke stack. But then I said, "If I pick out a target to get to the hole, I'll end up guiding my swing, and that isn't release."

Mike asked me another question, "Why do you play this game?"

I then said to myself, "Why *do* I play this game?"

There was a pause, and then Mike said, "The purpose of the game is to get the ball in the hole." You know what? Mike said the hole is my target and that my target is larger than all the sand traps keeping me from my target.

"Why is it larger?" I asked.

He said it was because the professional mind-set is not worried about half of what is inside the amateur's mind-set.

"Do you mean," I asked him, "that the hole is not a glass darkly?"

He said, "That's exactly right." He went on to explain that the hole is the target that symbolizes that all trust is in darkness. There are no secrets. Golf is a simple game but we make it complicated.

For Mike, making the hole the target that empties out the traps and trees and water makes it possible to play without fear. Does that mean that, with God, all things are possible? When my friend Tom struck that ball into the water, it showed that he had let fear creep into his psyche. When I struck the ball, I guided my shot. I was hanging on when my ball avoided the water. Mike, on the other hand, doesn't have half in his mind and heart that which was distracting Tom and me. He knew better than we that the hole, which was his target, had already consumed that which was negative inside the rest of us. Mike had already emptied out the water hazards and sand traps, which were still inside us. Release, I came to understand, is the knowing that transforms the glass darkly into light. St. Paul reminds us that even if at first we don't see clearly, someday we will see. And when we do, all will be light.

Earlier in the round, Mike missed a putt that would have halved a six-hole match we were playing. I told Mike that we would have not lost the match if he had made that putt. Mike asked, "Why didn't you tell me?"

I said, "I didn't want to put any pressure on you."

Mike laughed and said, "I love the pressure. The pressure makes the target larger." In other words, the target is greater the more you understand that pressure is what the spirit allows to empty out your heart so that you can believe you are loved by God. Mike loves pressure because the outside and inside can destroy the darkness and make him a real witness of truth. Mike knows how to live on the release side of himself, especially on the golf course. When he plays he is in heaven.

Could it be that Adam and Eve's sin became pressure on the human family that kept them from believing God loved them. Maybe pressure made the target too small for our ancestors. Like golfers, our ancestors had to learn to believe that all love is in darkness. They too had to empty out the glass darkly inside them so they could see the target growing larger. Truth set them free when they let the journey into light come to them. Golf is a game that teaches you that it's possible to face your pressures. Pressure, if you learn to accept it as the spirit emptying out your heart, can reveal a much larger heart, which isn't worried about half of what is bothering the world. Release is what it means to know that heart—a heart that can close the deal on pressure and reveal God's love. This love can conquer all that distracts our mind-sets the way the black hole in golf is transformed into light by the likes of players like Mike Wynn, Tiger Woods, and Lee Trevino. All players I have mentioned in this book who continue to play the game of golf as a journey into light keep on releasing to be seeds for others. It's interesting that Tiger Woods even has the *Target* department store as one of his sponsors.

That day on the course with Tom, Charlie, and Mike, I began to see God's love increasing in my life. The target began to swallow up my darkness. I started to empty out my glass darkly and to reject intimidation from the pressure. Pressure will be there in life. We can't escape it. Pressure is our original sin. Having to live on the edge is our original sin. But, because the genius of Almighty God, whoever or whatever creates pressure doesn't know how to think out of the box. They don't know how to recognize the target that grows larger. Only the spirit who searches out our hearts possesses this knowledge. It's a knowledge in which commitment and discipline are combined into one entity. I mention commitment because belief in the truth is already there, and discipline because, to know the truth, you have to pay attention while you are emptying out your heart of your glass darkly.

That day with Mike, I took the pictures that are inside this book. Pay particular attention to Mike's right foot. Notice how Mike doesn't come up on his right toe until well after the clubhead is past his body. His clubface doesn't turn him from behind the ball in the traditional sense; Mike is behind the ball but only because the ball is in front of him. He manages to keep his setup on this side of the ball by turning and returning squarely through impact. Mike never gets ahead of square but maintains his height through the shot so that square can release through the hitting area. Mike's swing incorporates the principles of the long drivers today, but, for Mike, it's not about muscle. It's about release inside a long driver's setup. Remember, Mike Wynn is 5'5" tall, and he hit the ball close to 270 yards. When you study these pictures, it's important that you extend your arms away from the ball. I then understood and stood away from the ball as behind it. I let my arms hang extended from my shoulders back, turned my shoulders with my spine, let the handle go around the spine with my hands. I saw immediate improvement and lowered my handicap from 7 to 5. For the first time, I didn't hit the ball. I maintained my height and kept the ball in front of me. I didn't strike the ball with my hands. Everything struck the ball, and, you know what, my right foot stayed down until well after impact. I didn't transfer my weight from right to left. I turned my hips because I kept the ball in front of me. I didn't push off my right foot to hit the ball. I released the shot. It was exciting. But it wasn't the shot that excited me. It was recognition of my target getting larger.

After this, the journey in golf was beginning to make sense as part of my life. I only had to learn to wait for people like Mike Wynn to be the notes in my life to make the journey an epiphany.

At this point, I'd like to mention my mother, Ann Steib, the only person in my family to have her name on the championship board at Evergreen Country Club in Haymarket, Virginia, where I am very proud to be a member. By my mother's example, she has been able to teach me much about *release*. In fact, she is Finnish, and in Finland they have a word they use to express release. It's *sisu*. Well, my mom definitely has *sisu* and continues to pass it onto me.

I hope you have experienced some *sisu* after reading this book. But if you haven't, that's OK, too. Maybe someday we will meet again and realize we are on the journey together. The journey we travel is not its own destination. It's a revelation of the kingdom of God within us, which we are called to witness so that evil will not overpower us and so God's favor will be done on earth as it is in heaven.

Biography

Bart Steib is the author who holds a Bachelor's Degree in Physical Education from the College of William and Mary and a Master's Degree in Interdisciplinary studies from the University of Oregon. Bart has been a golfing member at Evergreen Country Club in Haymarket, Virginia for thirty-three years. Bart is an eight handicap who recently won the 2004 Washington Catholic Athletic Coach's tournament.

978-0-595-33853-5
0-595-33853-4

Printed in the United States
35501LVS00007B/229-243